DALÍ

Ramón Gómez de la Serna

DALÍ

PARK LANE
New York

Editor: FRANCO PAONE
Design: BRUNO ACQUALAGNA and WALTER PREGNOLTO
Translated from the Spanish by: NICHOLAS FRY
Translated from the Italian by: ELISABETH EVANS
Frontispiece: RAMÓN GÓMEZ DE LA SERNA, collage by SALVADOR DALÍ

This edition is published by Park Lane, a division of Crown Publishers,
Inc.
a   b   c   d   e   f   g   h
Library of Congress Catalog Card Number 79-52287

*Printed and bound in Italy by officine Grafiche di Arnoldo Mondadori Editore,
Verona*

Contents

Our introduction to Salvador Dalí in this book takes the form of an essay by Ramón Gómez de la Serna, who knew the artist in Madrid in the 1920s. At Ramón's death it was still unfinished and was the fruit of his lasting appreciation of Dalí rather than any personal friendship, although Dalí had promised to illustrate the biography when it finally appeared as a book. He kept this promise thirty years later when the manuscript was found among the author's papers after his death, together with other short notes on surrealism, on Dalí, on soft clocks, and a certain powerfully ambiguous verse entitled "Dalí Rhinoceros": "The whole world / is as beautiful / as a rhinoceros."

After this introductory essay there are seventy-eight reproductions of Dalí's work, together with a note on his relationship with Ramón Gómez de la Serna, a chapter on the Dalí Theater Museum at Figueras, a chronology of the artist's life and work, a recent interview with Dalí, and a collection of accounts by Dalí himself, by André Breton, the leader of the surrealist movement, and by one of the leading authorities on surrealism.

The Right to
the Imagination and
to Madness

"That Youthful Genius Who Fills the Showcase of the World"

Essay by Ramón Gómez de la Serna

We must be careful not to say too much about the painter, for it is in our honour, and for our edification, that he uses up his vital substance.

Bernard Shaw once said: "One uses mirrors to look at one's face and Art to look at one's soul."

Thus painting is an eternal putting on of masks; its appearances are of the strangest and its different faces shock.

It is easy to call an extraordinary artist mad, but difficult to prove it, and Dalí in any case has an answer to the charge: "The only difference between me and a madman is that I am not mad." The nearest he comes to madness is in his imitation of it in his "paranoiac-critical" period, which he has described as "a spontaneous method of irrational knowledge, based on the interpretive-critical association of delirious phenomena."

Dalí is a pure Catalán, full of that matutinal magnificence which is only to be found in Catalonia and which I have so often savoured with admiration and fraternal recognition. We must remember this fact, for it is the main source of that amazing adolescence, of the prolific output of that youthful genius who fills the showcase of the world, much to the world's amazement, who moves even the cranes and giraffes of New York, who influences even that superabundant capital of civilization.

Dalí, with that great Spanish dignity which admits of no plagiarism, owes nothing to Picasso in his work, absorbing only the natural influence of everything modern on a renewed originality.

Dalí is the child of a new species.

He was born in Figueras, Catalonia, on May 11, 1904.

He studied in Madrid, and we may gather from his lucid and by no means obscure utterances that he admired Meissonier and sniffed the malvaceous effusions of Mariano Fortuny, a delirious painterly talent of the nineteenth century.

Dalí's great instinct is for preserving his infantile impressions intact, with all their insights; he is quick to seize, and to release, the things which attract him, faster and franker than anyone to the minute, five thousand revolutions of times more than anyone else.

Dalí was a unique adolescent who has remained an adolescent.

Dalí represents the desire for total extravagance which exists in every generation and which presupposes sacrifice, martyrdom, and terror in the soul. It is a desire which burns much fuel in a few years, and Dalí, who is very young, appears very old. But this is something which does not bother him, for as he himself has said numerous times, he desires old age—that category of being which is much respected in China.

It is on these renewers of art and actuality that working in the world takes its most terrible toll; for this reason there have been, and are, so many hemiplegic painters. "The nothingness with which the painter begins in space ... the space which is the nothingness which envelops every object in the world, caressing it and strangling it at the same time"—it is from this nothingness that Dalí has done everything. And he strives to make this work on reality mysterious, scabrous, and disconcerting.

Dalí's eye is diamond-sharp.

The creed of Salvador Dalí is summarized in this litany which he heads with the battle cry "My struggle."

MY STRUGGLE

Against Simplicity	For Complexity
Against Uniformity	For Diversification
Against Egalitarianism	For Hierarchization

TRAJANO

13

Against the Collective	For the Individual
Against Politics	For Metaphysics
Against Music	For Architecture
Against Nature	For Esthetics
Against Progress	For Perenniality
Against Mechanism	For the Dream
Against Abstraction	For the Concrete
Against Youth	For Maturity
Against Opportunism	For Machiavellian Fanaticism
Against Spinach	For Snails
Against the Cinema	For the Theater
Against Buddha	For the Marquis de Sade
Against the Orient	For the Occident
Against the Sun	For the Moon
Against Revolution	For Tradition
Against Michelangelo	For Raphael
Against Rembrandt	For Vermeer
Against Savage Objects	For the Ultracivilized 1900 Objects
Against Modern Art	For the Art of the Renaissance
Against Philosophy	For Religion
Against Medicine	For Magic
Against Mountains	For the Coast Line
Against Phantoms	For Specters
Against Women	For Gala
Against Men	For Myself
Against Time	For Soft Watches
Against Skepticism	For Faith

Dalí focuses with more awareness than anyone else on the marginal world which had to be created so that we could divest ourselves of the essential monstrosity embodied in the mirage of mountains and people. Away with *bad objects!*

Thus he is the purest and most unrestrained man in existence, for he has done away with all aberrations and intrusive memories, and can walk light-footed and refreshed in front of his paintings.

Understanding things better can only do us good, for by worrying at things which we would do better to understand, we only foster a rodentlike mentality.

It is absurd that if a picture is not understood it is assumed to be lacking in meaning, and it never passes through the viewer's head that he could be the one who is lacking in understanding.

Dalí attacks with the aggressiveness of genius. He cannot discuss things seriously in the middle of a trivial conversation, because it would take too long and he would not be understood.

He insults, he creates, but he is not impertinent.

Cocteau was an ironist; he did not create, he *was* impertinent. "His mellifluous voice," he said of someone, "resembled those ridiculous curves of Art Nouveau," thinking that he had thus killed Art Nouveau. Dalí loves it and resuscitates it.

Dalí wants idealists who do not adhere to any ideal.

This must be my theme in drawing a profile of Dalí as a young lion, bathed in the clear matutinal light of Catalonia, on his return from an expedition to Paris with his parents.

One day, after an exhibition of incomprehensible pictures, his father, who was a widower, asked him what strange symbolism there could be in a painting which mocked his family.

"There's no symbolism," was the reply. "It's just what it seems."

The father immediately threw his son out of the house, and Dalí entered on his Calvary, alone and apparently bent on embracing his destiny—which is to redeem from prejudice the human being who wishes to rebel.

He was not afraid, because the worst had already happened to him. Soon the peaceful and beautiful city of Barcelona was in uproar; the council of the Ateneo Barcelonés resigned in a body, and indignantly recounted to me the cause of contention at a banquet which I attended in that august city at the time.

I didn't know what to say to them, and smiled, for I could see that this is the only way of travelling towards the future—by breaking down the existing horizon with outrage and abuse.

Dalí, in an excess of anxiety, was playing jokes on Spain. He appeared in Málaga with a garland of jasmine around his neck, and Gala had a fiesta bathing without a bathing suit on the primly clad beach. A few days more, while the *malagueños* were still realizing that their eyes had not deceived them, Dalí was already to be seen beside his fenestral paintings in Paris, revealing the photographic plates of his superior vision.

He painted faster than anyone had before, he was more outrageously daring, more technically skilled in anatomical, pictorial, and botanical terms. Not only did he invent all his monsters, he painted them in the most accomplished manner, sculpturally moulding their stumps of limbs and conveying the flabby quality of their time.

Dalí's art has its own particular strength, and so does psychoanalysis, yet no one can fail to be struck by the thesis and antithesis which they so obviously represent.

Dalí dissects reality and was the first artist who, in the face of the spiritless art of Picasso, gave effective expression to man's complexes and unsatisfied desires.

For this reason, Freud considered Dalí a great Spanish fanatic.

Art is one against all, an act of defiance in the face of the uncomprehending mass.

Art always stands above everything else, however high or low its point of departure.

Art is a lie which is superior to truth and truth which is superior to a lie.

When he was in New York, Dalí broke the window of a showcase containing his works—they were badly displayed—and was sent to jail. There he wrote a manifesto entitled "Declaration of Independence of the Imagination and Man's Right to Madness."

His basic and definitive ideas are contained in these few paragraphs, which appear in his marvellous autobiography: "There can be no intellectual greatness outside the tragic and transcendental sense of life: religion." Karl Marx wrote: "Religion is the opium of the masses." But history would demonstrate that his materialism would be the poison of "concentrated hatred" on which people would really croak, suffocated in the sordid, stinking, and bombarded subways of modern life. Whereas "the religious illusion" had made the contemporaries of Leonardo, of Raphael, and of Mozart thrill beneath the perfection of the architectonic and divine cupolas of the human soul!

"Mine was not a case of the periodic imitative and discouraged 'return to tradition'—the neoclassicism, the neo-Thomism—which one heard about everywhere, symptomatically arising out of the fatigue and the nausea over isms. On the contrary, it was the combative affirmation of my whole experience with the spirit of synthesis of the 'conquest of the irrational.' "

Courageous as he alone could be, he defended, from no less a place than North America, the idea of exclusivity over that of the lowest common denominator, for his cosmogony "is neither reaction nor revolution, but a Renaissance of hierarchy and an exclusive knowledge of everything."

"Postwar Europe had continually eaten isms and revolution. Its excrements henceforth would be war and death. The collective sufferings of the war of 1914 had led to the childish illusion of 'collective well-being,' based on the revolutionary abolition of all constraints. What had been forgotten was the morphological truth that is the very condition of well-being, which can only be ultra-individualistic and built on the rigor of hyperindividualistic laws and constraints capable of producing a 'form of reaction' original and peculiar to each spirit. Oh, the spiritual poverty of the postwar era, the poverty of individual formlessness swallowed up in the formlessness of the masses! The poverty of a civilization which, avowedly destroying every kind of constraint, becomes the slave of the skepticism of its new liberty, constrained to the most practical and the basest necessities, those of the mechanical and industrial type! The poverty of a period that replaces the divine luxury of architecture, the highest crystallization of the material liberty of intelligence, by 'engineering,' the most degrading product of necessity! The poverty of a period which has replaced the unique liberty of faith by the tyranny of monetary utopias! . . . The responsibility of the war which was to break out would lie solely on the ideological poverty, the spiritual famine of this postwar period, which had mortgaged all its hopes on bankrupt materialistic and mechanical speculations."

In the future, people will look for a Dalí as they look for a Patinir, among the major paintings of their time.

For only an angel could paint like he does and write: "And what is heaven? Where is it to be found? Heaven is neither above nor below, neither to the right nor to the left, heaven is to be found exactly in the centre of the bosom of the man who has faith!"

In the meantime, Dalí triumphed in the "promised land" of North America, sold every painting for at least $15,000 and, whereas Picasso divorced his wife so as not to have to buy her a Hispano-Suiza automobile, Dalí unexpectedly presented Gala with a Cadillac and carried on their idyll, now and then exclaiming: "My God, how lucky neither you nor I am Rodin!"

Ivan Goll will help me to paint a few scenes from his life and say some other things about him. Dalí visited Freud in London, and painted a portrait of him which is the most accurate imaginable. He even garnered a memorable phrase from him: "In classic paintings, I look for the subconscious—in a surrealist painting, for the conscious."

That day fixed Dalí's conversion. He returned to the pure tradition of the Spanish painters—that of violence and passion. After El Greco and Goya, after Juan Gris and Picasso, he was to mix on his pallet the blood of the Lord and the red of his Catalonian soil.

His ecstatic realism recalled that of Valdés Leal, of the Church of Charity in Seville, who did not shrink from painting the worms and slime of his corpses. In *The Face of War* the skulls of the dead in turn produce an infinity of blind or one-eyed skulls in the horrified eyes of their progeny.

Snobs of the world are perpetually waiting for the latest school from Paris: it has to be a school since novelty does not triumph in the same way in the form of an individual work.

If Paris is not to grow old before its time, if it is not to consist solely of the dead and dying, it needs to maintain the heroism of new schools, to persist in the pursuit of novelty.

The dawn of a new school always has the air of a shipwreck on the Seine. In a solemn and terrible moment, a few young desperadoes who have already had to commit suicide once come forth in a body to find salvation, and standing bloody and scratched on the Pont Neuf, shout their watchword like the lottery seller offering today's tickets.

Like everything that happens at dawn, no one can see the colour of the ticket until more time has passed, when the colour of anticipation becomes the colour of speculation, and then, as happens with every new school, hesitation turns to commitment.

This time it was the brides of Dadaism who were left in the street, their veils askew like those ants that lose their wings after the nuptial flight.

The year 1921 was about to sound and surrealism appeared as "a glorious body for the use of mankind."

The fundamental part of its announcement and doctrine is in my *Ismos* (Isms); but as I never repeat myself, here are a few flashbacks, some illuminating glimpses of what went on.

Every attempt at treading a new path, every new complex of assumptions, has its own particular name and produces its own line of harebrained projects, its own original collection of outrages and scandals, all of which must be borne philosophically, for art is never a crime.

Everyone, we maintain, is entitled to his own opinion, but while most of us would support those who share our enthusiasms, we have little time for tastes which are diametrically opposed to our own.

These youngsters taking their turn thumbing their noses at the world were obviously not "our kind of people."

They were reacting against the common herd, and could almost say, with the Tao-te Ching:

> *When everyone in the*
> *world understands*
> *that beauty is*

good, then
ugliness exists.
Thus, wisdom
does its work without
action, and gives its teaching
without words.

André Breton succinctly described what it was all about: "Surrealism does not use the pretext of art—for which read antiart—to concern itself with philosophy or antiphilosophy; in other words, it is interested in nothing which does not aim at the annihilation of being in a blind and brilliant intimacy, which is not the soul of the mirror or of fire."

Like so many others before them, they brought out high-sounding phrases, proclaiming the "creation of a new kind of mysticism," announcing that they wished "to restore to thought its original purity and put an end to the civilization you are so fond of."

They wished to avoid coercing that which emerges from the human subconscious, favouring automatic writing and somnambulism, which enabled them to use their dreams creatively, not converting the products of dreaming into picturesque cleverness, but approaching dreams without any preconception of their outcome.

They announced another artistic extravagance which they called "the extraordinary ordinary," maintaining that "the strange sensations which a man can experience, faithfully reproduced by himself, can bring new pleasures to a sensitive and intelligent person."

They were in love with cosmic temptation: surprise was for them the "passional element." They favoured the objective force of chance which when allied to the subconscious produces hallucination.

They argued the merits of hazard and logic; for them imagination was an indication of what might be.

They dabbled in esotericism, seeing themselves as "masters," and ... one step further and they had fallen into theosophy.

They believed in phantasms, in the soul of palaces, and ... one step further and they had fallen into spiritualism.

They took it in turns to frighten one another, and Chirico, walking with Breton through Versailles, discovered that "every corner of the palace, every column, every window, has a soul which is an enigma."

They saw themselves as clairvoyants, and cited the case of the painter Brauner, who had painted a self-portrait with one eye, although he had two, until one day he really lost one in a surrealists' quarrel. Then there was Apollinaire, who had a bas-relief portrait of himself with a wound in the forehead, which became reality in the 1914–18 war when he was wounded by a shell fragment in exactly the same place.

Besides these cogitations over the magical and fakirical, they practiced psychoanalysis. Breton, who had studied medicine, met Freud in 1917 and practiced his doctrines on the war-wounded in the hospital.

For the writer, this search into the real depths of man is a process of entanglement and disentanglement in the morass of human life.

As always happens in these great Paris confections, the ingredients included both poets and painters. The group had declared its intention of effecting a "change of life," and this change applied to painting as much as anything else.

They supported "objective chance," and Breton even said that "the painter can only paint surprises."

Giorgio de Chirico wrote: "It must never be forgotten that a painting should always be the reflection of a deep sensation, which means a strange one, and strange means little known, or completely unknown."

Surrealism turned into one more license to investigate the original, a license for the painter to try to paint something more than insincere trifles.

It is only the antipodeans of the art scene who get drunk on naval whisky and paint automatically in a state of hope.

Like the surrealist writers, the painters concentrated their attention on the objects which proliferated in their subconscious like sponges in the sea.

It was essentially on the object—as Breton said—that surrealism had fixed its lucid gaze in recent years. Surrealism was in fact a close examination of various recent speculations on the nature of this object (the dream object, the symbolically functioning object, the real and virtual object, the mobile, microcosmic object, the object rediscovered, etc.), carried out with the aim of finding a direction for the movement.

Breton's guide in this elevation of the *object* was Marcel Duchamp, who in 1911 had already raised a coffee mill to pictorial prominence and canonized a bristling bottle brush—a line which was later to culminate in his birdcage with pieces of marble distributed like sugar lumps and a thermometer inserted between the wires, bearing the title "Why Not Sneeze?"

The ready-made was ready and the first surrealist exhibition was celebrated with all due joyousness and outrage. It was surrealism's great day of celebration, after the provocative shows in one of which someone shouted "It's raining on a skull" every four seconds, causing such indignation among the audience that they threw small change, followed by eggs, which the surrealists declared "produced a wonderful decorative effect."

The exhibition was in darkness and one was guided through it by gentlemen with pocket flashlights wearing no tie but white gloves, who revealed live snails on wax décolletés, chests of drawers overflowing with legs and mousetraps. Serendipity was the keynote to this jovial display among the grottoes of the Luna Park, in every corner of which was a spider or a trident. Sacks of coal hung from the ceiling of the exhibition sprinkling black dust on the spectators, and the smell of roasting coffee wafted through every room, while a voice issued from some hidden cabinet, uttering muffled cries and offering insults to familiar faces.

It was the period in which anything and everything was suggested—an exhibition of lepers from Madagascar with vitamins doled out to students and watercolours painted by the obese. It was the time when they noticed that the atom bomb at Hiroshima had snatched the shadow off a man who was crossing a bridge with a little cart—disposing of his shadow before destroying the man himself.

Everything went well until political extremism became involved and André Breton declared himself inclined to make way for the "definitive diversion of the forces of intellect in favour of revolutionary fatality."

Picasso, who is the "permanent revolution" of painting, reaffirmed his support of Breton; but after the syndication came Trotsky's persecution, and as the two of them were Trotskyites, they found themselves out on a limb; surrealism fragmented and Breton was left with one or two diehards. But for a while the group had been entertained by Dalí's facility and his "paranoiac-critical" theorizing.

The rout continued. Chirico returned to tradition and disowned his geometer's manikins, Aragon obeyed Russia. Dalí broke free and found success in New York, for which he earned—undeservedly—the name of Avida Dollars from Breton.

Occasionally sparks of the old fire would reappear, and when Tristan Tzara spoke at the Sorbonne, Breton and his remaining disciples went along to shout: "Aren't you ashamed to be talking in a place like this?"

All that remained of the school were the poets—of the poets themselves, Breton, Eluard, Peret, and of the painters, the Spaniard Miró, standing firm as he alone could, keeping on his mask, heroically taking the strain.

Joan Miró, with his air of an astonished Catalán peasant, of an unconquered gardener, of a rustic floriculturist, was the faithful surrealist who would not take a single step further than he could think.

Only he knew the balance of his piscicological signs painted in the sky and on the earth, over Mediterranean blues which consoled him for living in Paris.

Circus figures, Catalán peasants in disguise, and performing dogs were mixed with trapeze artists and high-wire acrobats trying to reach their meridian hanging from the ceiling.

He persevered with his horned graffiti—suggestions of mud walls traced with a chalk or burnt stick by some anonymous child—exposing himself to all the severity of criticism or astonishment—even unto death!

He went on writing love letters in the surrealist style and ate bow nets as if they were fish, perhaps insoluble but none the less edible.

He was the intrepid fly fisherman, casting his synthetic lures, knowledgeable about the hook and the curved feather, filling his paintings with the coloured tails of his craft.

His was the motto "Never apologize, never explain," the shapes he painted were beyond comparison or counterreformation—the work neither of children nor of lunatics nor of painters who paint with figurative remnants.

His objects evoke nothing—not laboratory compounds, not microbes, nothing—yet they balance each other within the confines of the canvas in a way which is unique to him.

Max Ernst, Tanguy, and a few others capered around him, but the one true artist was this parsimonious Catalán who refused to be questioned by the critical police.

"What is it?" they asked.

"It is what it is," came the reply.

All those photomontages and collages, the deserts in which stones and maggots, caterpillars of camels, lead towards the Mecca of surrealism—all these smack of the anecdotal, but in Miró there is not a crack where it can infiltrate.

Miró was an artist completely committed to surrealism, who would have gone to the gallows without saying a word in self-defense, without buttonholing his critics and trying to persuade them of the rightness of his views.

The surrealist manifestos are now little more than

faded records of past history, and the only things which have survived are the images to be found in its anthologies and its dictionary ("my room is enlarged by a torn-open envelope," "the lion's claw squeezes the heart of the vineyard").

The men who wanted to revise history will themselves be revised, those who put Barrès on trial will be convicted; those who said "All writing is rubbish" will be criticized, and those who spat on Poe will suffer the same injustice.

They have already been abashed by the way psychoanalysts have gone on to achieve their own success, with their clinics and their confessional couches, with their numerous publications full of elucidatory articles, investigating the uninvestigable.

Superpsychiatry produces writing which is not automatic but traumatic, fusiform, written from the groin.

Breton has grown old, he wears a long raincoat and sits on benches in the long tree-lined boulevards like a tired angel—fatherhood has humanized him—and doesn't feed the birds, having not forgotten that it was he who said: "Down with those who scatter cursed bread to the birds!"

Max Jacob, that beneficent martyr, had said: "Art stops being very modern when the person who is producing it starts to understand it; when those who could understand it and those who have understood it start to look for an art which they will never understand."

Finally existentialism, the other swing of the pendulum, the negative side, appeared just as surrealism was looking for something positive, had to come in from the deep sea and touch bottom.

It was the face of Dada again, but fiercer, more grotesque, like the gargoyles of Paris, more satanic, more shabby than before.

It was the same Paris fair ground as before, the same merry-go-round, with new stalls and sideshows.

The artist was clad in the same drab colours as the walls of the time, a shabby dandy, distinguished yet hidden in the crowd. He was a faded scarecrow, giving off a suggestion of softness which compensated for the extravagance of his character, a necktie sometimes providing the only gaudy note in his attire.

His living came from the old-clothes shop, not from the brightly coloured rags of the remnant sale.

The existentialists, having come to art unexpectedly, ignored the *noblesse oblige* of the bohemian and indulged in some outrageous tartan shirts of would-be sporting cut which the makers had been unable to get rid of except by indulging in degrading wholesale transactions, having overestimated the number of enthusiasts for their multicoloured creations.

These brightly checked shirts filled the display windows shortly after the war and seemed designed to preclude any possibility of their being adopted by fascists, antifascists, or neotenists, suitable only for the hopeless cases.

Then the existentialists appeared and bought the lot at half price.

Their choice of shirts alone made them suspect, inspiring little confidence in those who could read the signs.

There was something hasty and disorientated about the youngsters' choice of these frivolous, nondescript, daytripper's shirts. It gave them the image of a movement of bargain hunters, and the fact that their garments lasted longer than before made them appear even more meretricious than the rest.

Sitting ostentatiously on the café terraces and drinking that light French beer which tastes of hops and barley water—the most innocuous beer in the world—they looked like globetrotters of the American Northwest, with a suggestion of the cyclist or the shopkeeper.

The shirt cult of the existentialists added a suggestion of frivolity to that inconsistent school, diluting the austerity of the doctrine which had come before—surrealism.

Picasso, who was, or could have been, the paternal admonisher of those who had strayed into excessive unorthodoxy, could not intervene in this vestimentary dispute, since he himself had lapsed into another sartorial absurdity more related to the beach than to the atelier: the shorts and beach shoes which he had taken to wearing in his comfortable living room and the intimacy of his studio or garden on the Côte d'Azur.

This playboy's outfit did not suit him either, and as his shorts were white and baggy they tended to crease, taking on the appearance of some outlandish piece of underwear.

Casually attired and casual in approach, cubism and existentialism lacked the artistic and dramatic excellence which we expect of the truly heroic schools.

So one had to put up with Picasso in his golfer's shorts from Golfe Juan, and the existentialists in their picnicker's getup, taking time out from their picnic in the cafés of Paris, which always seem to partake of the atmosphere around the tote board at a race meeting.

Apart from this, existentialism was a step backwards, a fashionable diversion, but its audience of atheists and heavy wine drinkers willingly rejected all the grandeur of

23

mystery and immortality in favour of the eternal life of an *hôtel meublé* smelling of dust and old carpets. Stand-up comics and popular songsters welcomed it as the latest trend and sang the charming existentialist song about "the woman with the navel shaped like a 5" (why not a 6?).

The new high priest turned against surrealism, "destroying everything real, destroying itself with it."

That young existentialist Henri Calar de Bear who planned to dynamite the Eiffel Tower did not know what he was doing. He was unable to tell the difference between the new and enigmatic and the old and vulgar.

He was one of those people who dismiss anything strange as vulgar. He failed to appreciate the abstract grandeur of that scaffold rising between the earth and the sky.

I have always admired that great Paris landmark and its inventor, Gustave Eiffel, whose three-hundred-meter inspiration rose in the Champ de Mars as the ideal advertisement for the Paris Exhibition of 1889.

An engineer and a gentleman who always wore a top hat, only he could have thought of building a structure that high.

He had already built numerous bridges, swivelling roofs for astronomical places, and elevators like the one in Lisbon, which seems to transport us to the streets of paradise. But his great aspiration to the Olympus of fame was the Parisian tower, a tower of Babel in miniature which rises layer upon layer to the sky, as if in exposition of all the problems which there have been and will ever be.

The assassin of the Eiffel Tower had no idea what he was taking on, since among the unforeseen merits of the tower were that it invented the aerial before the wireless—which is why Paris was and is a major radio transmission center—and that the first airplanes seemed to have hatched from the tower at its summit.

What a responsibility for a nineteen-year-old with more arrogance than sense!

Nothing seemed to worry him—the people in the restaurant, the postcard sellers, the guards in the radio station. Everything was going to be felled like the tallest of trees in a din of collapsing metal as if the very axis of the globe had broken.

He was going to set the whole thing swinging, and its lift—a cradle full of tourists—would fall as from the broken bough of the nursery rhyme.

It was all a bad dream, inspired by the rage of the small man against the great achievement, of the failure against a universally acclaimed success—and one which carried the best illuminated advertisements ever seen, lighting up the night sky of Paris.

The building with the biggest bird's-eye view in the world was going to die—swarming with tourists at the summit of their touristic careers, who would perish instead of cherishing the memory of their visit.

The great metal giraffe was going to bend its long neck and fall, knocking down houses and guillotining many of the people scattered around its base.

What an awakening there would be for Paris without its pride and joy, without the most existentialist of monuments deprived of its existence by some miserable sectarian of a dead idea.

The deed would not make the assassin famous, for when the Eiffel Tower fell it would be Eiffel who would rise from the wreckage, his name made glorious by his martyrdom.

But the tower, the toast of the exhibition and the monumental thermometer of Paris's dreams in the bedchamber of its panorama, that immense A which watched over one's astonished arrival in Paris and one's final departure, seemed to have received notice of the attack which the existentialists were planning via some subtle telepathic antenna, and informed the police, perhaps through an innate sympathy between its winding gear and their bicycles. And the police detained the conspirators, who were soon behind bars, unable to see the Great Tower of Paris, that emblem of modernism which was beyond their comprehension and which, through having been so often reproduced as a souvenir paperweight, had lost its air of a monumental candlestick with its radiant halo, standing at the center of the world.

Surrealism was destined to become connected with another doctrine, superior and more modern, which had nothing of the monstrous crudity of Sartrian existentialism.

It could be said to have stopped, stagnated, the tank of novelty bogged down in the trenches of the last war, even though, like the tanks, it might suddenly give a tremor and lumber on its way again.

And there it still is, its power hermetically sealed in the well-plowed earth of the present.

VELAZQUES

The last war threw everything into confusion, failing to produce the desired result of peace in victory square. If the result had not been confusion, if we had seen time set in motion again towards more progressive goals, surrealism would have continued its course, would have thrown open its ports and hatchways and laid claim to the new portion of evolution which was its due.

But instead everything stagnated, frozen by the cold war, the storm continued, terrible plumes of cloud swept across the sky.

Nevertheless surrealism, though stagnant and blunted, has not yet expired, and no one has been able to defuse the bomb it still carries in its belly.

It is still there with the driver of its tank talking through the eye slit, a little subdued at so much time's having passed without the fulfillment of his prophesies, a little lonely at the desertion of one or two of his group, and because so many of his potential disciples have been carried off by that glib and monstrous pedagogue called Sartre.

Some tailor or other, some strabismic confectioner of ill-fitting garments, has taken advantage of the situation and gathered his most disoriented disciples from the sidewalk cafés.

Nevertheless, the adventure of surrealism continues, and quite recently a bookshop displaying the *Anthology of Black Humour*—the humour preached by Breton the strict ex-communicant—filled its window with those alarm clocks in which a cobbler hammers a shoe, a bird pecks away the seconds, or a child plays on a seesaw.

In an interview with the writer José Maria Valverde, Breton replied to the question, What is the future of surrealism? by saying, "A fine painting by Picasso, dated 1913 (it was the period of the beginnings of aviation), has as its title one of the slogans of the day: Our future is in the air.

"There are ideas which are 'in the air' and which no one can prevent being realized once they have found their medium of expression."

Breton remains a great writer and poet, an oracle of our times who still has much to say. We may imagine him seated in his armchair surrounded by the large collection of paintings which are a legacy of his long apostolate, a souvenir which may perhaps console him for the apostasy of those who painted them.

The artist has to exploit his disillusionment, for Art is a form of hope in which there is no hope.

Surrealism has come a long way since its birth and has little to do with the first word which the infant uttered as it began to speak in 1916—Dada-Dada. "It said Dada, but it means Papa," said surrealism and adopted the child, even though it had come after the child.

The first official manifesto of surrealism appeared in 1924, but Breton had made reference to it previously, while the first to do so was Apollinaire, who mentioned it in passing even before his *Mamelles de Tirésias,* which he described as a surrealist drama. Surrealism was after all another way of practicing poetry. Only fragments of the manifestos now remain.

Breton said in his First Manifesto of Surrealism: "I believe in the future resolution of these two states, so contradictory in appearance, which are dream and reality, in a form of absolute reality, of super-reality, if we may call it that.

"I am on my way to conquering it, sure of never arriving but too unconcerned by my death not to think a little of the joy of such an achievement." It was Breton again who wrote in the Second Manifesto of Surrealism (1930): "Everything leads us to believe that there exists a certain point in the mind from which life and death, the real and the imaginary, the past and the future, the communicable and the incommunicable, the high and the low, cease to be perceived as opposites. It would be vain to seek in surrealist activity any other motive than the hope of determining this point."

The current image of surrealism is much more forceful, more dismissive, more poised between life and death, more scornfully precognizant of revolutionary change. It suggests the sudden insight of the man who is about to die.

Surrealism is a glimpse of the unheard-of, the geometry of the mind with its thousands of half-formed images, a geometry of as yet unknown laws, apparently superfluous planes, phantasmagorical architecture.

It is the reflection of the grotesque and the insane—a concentration of madness, the conception of the inconceivable. It is nothing to do with the poet as creator, that dwarflike figure of conventional art; it is a mental morass which throws up new ways of looking at reality.

Naturally, it contains an element of Luciferian ambition to create beauty instead of copying it. God created beauty, God created the first Venus, and since then every sculptor and every poet has merely copied the model which was God's creation.

Reacting against this fatal penchant for plagiarism, the surrealists succeeded in producing an art as pure as that of the insane, taking their cue from the decor of paranoia, in which, as they said, objects "come out disc-shaped."

The struggle is between life as a museum and museums as life. Life reflects, unable to decide whether it should become a museum and acquire official status, or continue being life, crude and simple.

One vague definition of surrealism was that it was a "purely physical automatism, through which it was proposed to express, either verbally or in writing, the real essence of thought." Painting also availed itself of this definition and devoted itself to pure, mystical intuition.

The irreconcilable was reconciled, even if the spectator was not.

Everything was mixed: the pretemporal and the nontemporal, chance and the subconscious, a whole phenomenalism without God. (Dalí has already reached God.)

Surrealism was a series of attempts at an esthetic, but not a complete system.

The movement was as much political as literary, and only its leader could not put himself beyond the pale by becoming a dissident from himself.

But away with these niceties! All the phenomena of transformation of death are surrealist—the sunken eyes, the made-up face, the coagula from the nose, the increasing odoriferousness of the most highly perfumed of corpses.

Everything is deformed by its own ephemerality, and it is this which the surrealists show, invested with a degree of artistry and elegance, bringing us face to face with the disintegration of death itself, a purely surrealist phenomenon.

"Where did you learn how to paint this?"

"Not in any academy."

"Then who gave you permission to paint it?"

"Death, which is Surrealist."

And so the years passed, and surrealism progressed, though naturally any new ideal could take its inspiration from the accumulation of material in the aging infant's toy cupboard.

Slowly the dream images faded with the memory of nights past, all the repressions had been brought out and their expression could hardly impress the current generation, and "black humour" nearly closed the cafés, since social intercourse may thrive on black coffee but not on humour of the same colour.

The original explanations fell out of use, and older

antecedents were found, such as the much-quoted Lau-tréamont.

The poets now realized that the basic principle of surrealism had been reached even before the arrival of the babbling infant Dada; Rimbaud's association of the auditory and the visual: "A, black; E, white; I, red; O, blue; U, green," is already an example of the surrealist penchant for arbitrary correspondences.

Just as incongruous were arguments such as that of the poem Ghil, who objected to Rimbaud's use of a composite colour like green and rectified the formula to "A, black; E, white; I, blue; O, red; U, yellow."

Thus surrealist writers and their antecedents were already using pictorial elements which were soon to be transformed into painting.

Even now, I still seem to see the amalgam of talents which gave those early days their character. Carrà, like an evening star, Chirico like some ancient ruin brought to life; Arp with his fragmented puzzle; Max Ernst with his scrambled advertisements, and Miró—I still remember that exhibition of his in which dry leaves made of wood veneer fluttered across skies of perfect blue, and seeing Gertrude Stein, who understood the great Spanish painter and used to buy his objects flying through purest space.

But the one figure who had not yet arrived was the Benjamin, the child prodigy of the whole movement, who would make it last longer than anyone else, the real entertainer of them all, Salvador Dalí, whom not even Tanguy could overshadow with his procession of boulders, representing the march of events, the changing landscape, and a general process of deterioration.

Dalí was one more representative of those convulsions to which Spanish painting is subject. The last convulsionist had been Picasso, always searching for something new.

The surrealist phenomenon emerges like some striving towards the beyond in the painting of every period—a landscape with a castle which on closer inspection turns out to be a bearded horseman—until in Hieronymus Bosch and his follower Brueghel it encompasses the earthly expanse between heaven and hell.

Goya, the great precursor of surrealism, came closest to surrealist invention in his etchings. A notable example are his birds with human heads, which were echoed by the woman's head in a birdcage displayed at the last surrealist exhibition with the slogan "At last the birds are caged."

Another Dalíesque invention consisting of a hat in the

form of a shoe echoes the theme of an etching which represents some women with a chair on their head and has the punning caption *"Ya tienen asiento"* ("They have a seat"/"They have reached the age of wisdom").

Dalí is a new leap forward, after that artistic athlete Picasso.

In *The Conquest of the Irrational,* Dalí says of his painting: "... How can you expect them to understand [my paintings] when I myself, who am their 'maker,' understand them as little. The fact that I myself at the moment of painting do not understand my own pictures does not mean to say that these pictures have no meaning; on the contrary, their meaning is so profound, complex, coherent, and involuntary that it escapes the most simple analysis of logical intuition. . . . My whole ambition in the pictorial domain is to materialize the images of concrete irrationality with the most imperialist fury of precision." If the Greeks nostalgically materialized their psychology and their Euclidian perceptions in the divine and muscular clarity of their sculptures, Salvador Dalí, in 1935, made use of the anxious questioning of Einsteinian space-time, not as an anthropomorphism, not as a libidinous arithmetic, not indeed as flesh at all. For Greek art is as different from Dalí's as chalk from cheese, and what after all are the famous soft watches of Salvador Dalí but a paranoiac-critical Camembert, soft, ripe, extravagant, alone in time and space?

Dalí is a noble figure because he supports all forms of renaissance, he accepts total mysteries and knows that the first surrealist objects were the ears and noses of the drawing schools, that the study materials of the anatomy classes are the key.

This was the period of his eyeballs without their whites, with the whole of the nervous and muscular system revealed to view, the period of his lightning compositions and the discovery of the soft watches showing the flaccid passage of time, which earned him the hatred of the Swiss watchmakers because they were unable to make them in their workshops.

Sometimes a man appears cruel, and yet he is a man who refuses to forget any of the things which have touched him, who seeks them unequivocally in the direct and the true, not in what he was told he ought to like, but in what appealed to him alone.

He worships the imaginary, the obsessive, the cock, the umbrella, the light table, the night table.

Dalí practices the artistic sublimation of his infantile desires, tribulations, and delights. (What he would most have liked to be is a kangaroo, especially since he is a painter and has nowhere to carry his paintboxes and sketchbooks.)

He has discovered a whole world and proclaimed its existence, he has expanded the stalactites of desire, and although his obsession with keys—which appear constantly in his work—is generally given a scatological interpretation, in fact they represent his great facility as the unlocker of ideas, associations of images, insinuations.

Having seen his early work as a naturalist painter, I know that he underwent a voluntary transfiguration as radical as if Velázquez had turned to cubism. Thus he heightens the impact of his subjects by his masterly painting of them, just as the poet adds to the impact of his theme by the quality of his verse.

But enough of these niceties of esthetic theorizing. The fact remains that one cannot live or think without surrealism and without what came afterwards and the hope of what is yet to come.

The surrealist approach to art, which as we know diverges somewhat from the figurative, has been justified by the overwhelming spread of colour photography, which renders every shade of colour and identifies its subjects with all the precision of a passport for the day of judgment, but cannot reproduce what lies behind what we see, that which is transformed into the art of today, that which is not there and which should be there. In the old style of painting there were those who painted happy days and those who painted sad days, but in the new we only find those who paint days beyond happiness and sadness. God is pleased with the new art because of its novelty and because the artistic without political or antireligious treacheries cannot possibly offend him.

The new art is the only real proof that civilization is evolving and changing, for its artists are creators and innovators, revealing the greater diversity which can be produced in the fantasies, the subconsciouses and the absurdities which lie beyond the immediate impression. For them the dome of many-coloured glass is shattered and we reveal ourselves to them through the half-open window between life and a notional beyond. They know the value of secret persuasion and their canvases are full of it. They call its silent hints to their aid, storing up materials for their future complexities, for they are well stocked compared with the painters of dead candles, pedestals of fallen wax surmounted by a moribund, lachrymal wick.

With their graphic conjuring and illusionism—the only fragment of creativity which man possesses—they demon-

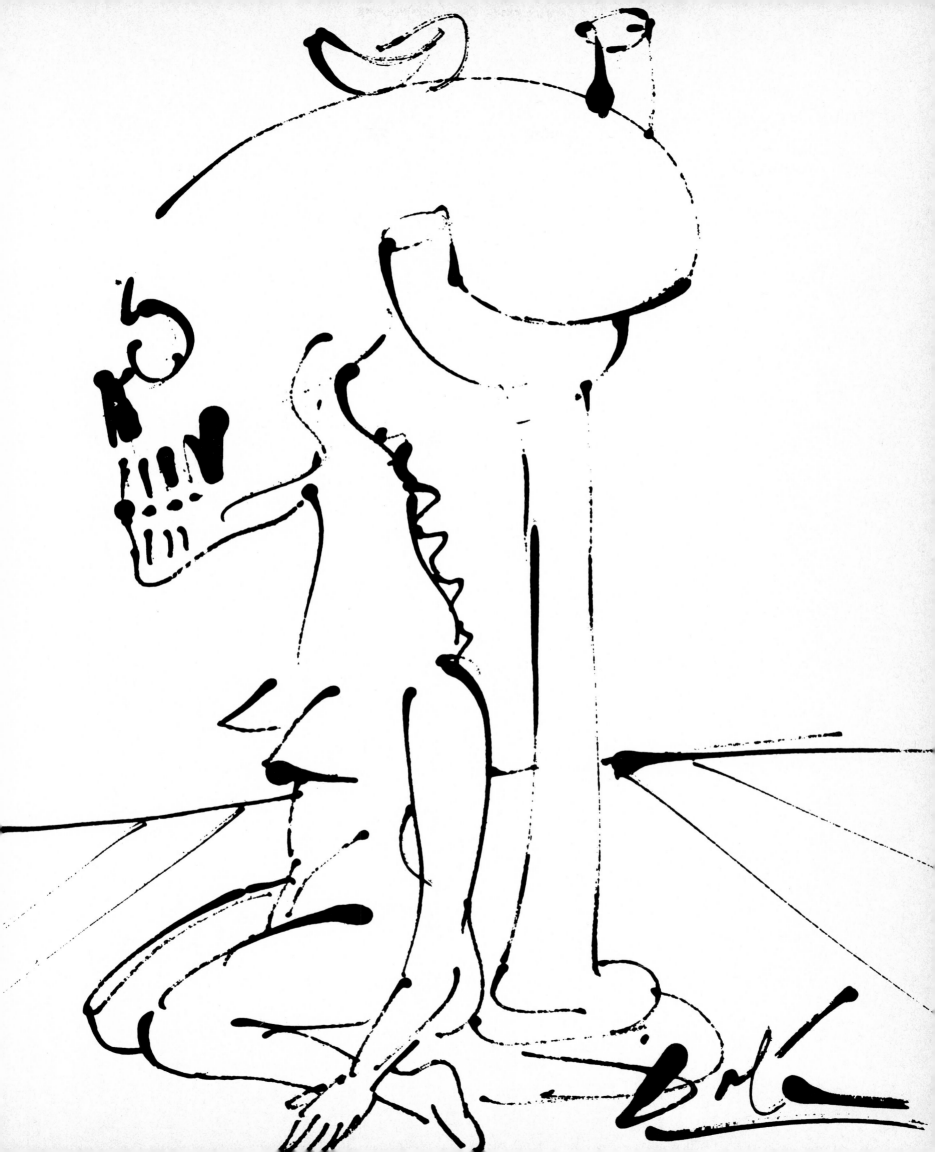

strate that the soul is immortal, because only an immortal soul can leave the solution of its hieroglyphics to the eternal world of the beyond. Each of the protagonists of this new art is different from the next, submitting to Baudelaire's maxim which says: "An artist, a man who is truly worthy of this great name, must possess something essentially *sui generis,* by virtue of which he is 'he' and not another."

The worst thing in life is the fact that it repeats itself, and the mission of art is to avoid this, eliminating monotony and giving respite from the crushing inertia of existence. We must accept the idea that painting should be more attractive, less anodyne, and more mysterious. Art is in essence a form of aspiration, seeking to mold the time which is as yet invisible, yet to come, the time of lives beyond our own. God created most things through art and for art—the earth, the heavens, and the stars. He need not have bothered with the stars, but he created them nevertheless, to fill the black emptiness of space.

Surrealism is not a joke, it is a superproduction, a horror show, a panic-stricken circumstance. Art is an opinion theorized to the farthest of the far beyonds, to the ultimate point of the best fiestas of the spirit which fearlessly transcend the dawning rays of the sun. Thus we who are dedicated to the elucidation of art climb the ladder of light which rises from the earth to the heavens.

The art of our time is an evolution towards greater risk-taking. Certainly isolated images presented to us by its painting are able to seize the unclouded consciousness and make it become one with them. Surrealism was a bridge between the real and the phantasmagorical, linking the physical and the metaphysical, all done in the manner of a sleepwalker who aims at a difficult target in which only a bull's-eye will open up landscapes and living anatomies. The images of surrealism are a multitude of superimpositions and transformations, the most heterogeneous selection of objects combined into allegory. For when its artists aimed true, "something" emerged—just as muses and monsters appear and trains and boats are set in motion in the magical atmosphere of the fairground.

Fundamentally they wanted to reveal that the most enlightening things in life are the unexpected ones.

Their canvases have the look of aircraft which have just arrived or are about to leave. They open up reality in another direction.

They seem enmeshed in terrible paradoxes, but this is by no means sure, for they are the supreme analogists.

Breton explained the matter admirably: "I never experienced intellectual pleasure outside the realms of analogy. For me the only certainty in the world is governed by the spontaneous, extralucid, insolent reaction which takes place under certain conditions between one thing and another which common sense would never prompt one to bring together; just as certainly as the most hateful word of all for me is 'Well . . . ,' with all the vanity and melancholy delectation which it implies. I love passionately everything which, randomly breaking the thread of discursive thought, suddenly takes off like a comet, lighting up a life of intensely fertile relationships, the secret of which was to all appearances known to primitive man. . . .

"The primordial contacts have been broken, and I maintain that only by means of analogy can these contacts be fleetingly reestablished. Hence the importance which these transient glimmers from the lost mirror occasionally acquire. . . . In common with mystical analogy, poetical analogy transgresses the laws of deduction to enable the mind to apprehend two objects of thought situated on different planes, between which the mind's logical function cannot establish a bridge, and indeed is *a priori* opposed to any kind of bridge being extended. Poetic analogy differs fundamentally from mystical analogy in that in no way does it presuppose an invisible universe tending to manifest itself through the fabric of the visible world. On the contrary, it is entirely empirical in its progress, for empiricism is the only thing which can ensure the total freedom of movement necessary for the jump which it has to make. If one considers its effects, it is true that poetic analogy, like mystical analogy, appears to support the concept of a world of infinite ramifications all nourished by the same sap, but while remaining independent of the sensible, i.e., sensual field, it shows no tendency to fall into the supernatural.

"Poetic analogy tends to afford glimpses of the true 'absent' life and an appreciation of its value, and given that it does not take any substance from metaphysical illusion, nor does it think of crediting any of its conquests to the glory of some hypothetical 'beyond.' "

All this to justify the production of monsters? Let us hear Baudelaire's defense of apparent deformity: "That which is not in some way deformed has something indefinably insensitive about it; as a result, irregularity, or rather the unexpected, surprise, admiration, are an essential part, and the most characteristic, of beauty." Many of its irregularities, its shorthand renderings of the vagaries of chance, are due to the pure mockery of "black humour" and for this reason its best journal is entitled *The*

Quadrilateral Triangle.

Art is impatience, sarcasm, instigation in the face of the slowness and vulgarity of life, and thus it is a slap in the face of the world.

Does this mean it is revolutionary politics?

No, it is certainly not!

We are merely seeing some artists offering new means of expression in order to break down the bourgeois rigidity of our habits.

One supporter of surrealism has explained this desire to change life very well: "These ideals, these modes of feeling, are fundamentally no different from what they were in the first formulation which I gave them. Always, it all comes down to the necessity of 'changing life.' More than ever this life which is forcing itself upon us is proving unacceptable: for quite a few years now there has been almost no one prepared to defend it.

"A large-scale operation is urgent and indispensable: it is all a question of knowing what kind of action must be taken. And to this surrealism has never ceased to reply that such action must be applied to the exterior world (its economic and social structure) and to the interior world— that is, to human understanding. Such indeed has been the opinion of both a reformer of genius such as Charles Fourier and a poet of genius such as Arthur Rimbaud. It need hardly be said that the characteristic activity of surrealism involves the interior world. Today it is well known that there has been no more often repeated proposition than that of freeing the spirit from the barriers of such opposites as 'action and dream,' 'reason and madness,' 'sensation and representation,' etc., which constitute the major obstacles of Western thought. What those artists are asking from me is the right to investigate the human problem in all its forms, the right to freedom of subject matter, the rejection of the principle that the quality of a work should be judged by the current extent of its public, resistance to everything which limits the intellectual's field of action and observation."

For me, Dalí, the man who hates spinach because it sticks to one's teeth, is the perfect renovator among artists, the most convincing representative of the new age.

I believed in Dalí from the moment he appeared, and for me he was a child who was beginning to play with the same things I had played with: wax dolls, plastic teaching materials, empty cages, etc., adding new and amazing toys which he had invented, such as myths without a mythology.

I always defend him, and for this reason when I heard people say he had become commercialized, I replied:

"It's not true . . . commerce has come to Dalí, the dealers have been Dalified."

We share the same attitude towards life, the same political and religious ideas, have taken the same way of independence.

When he was in New York he agreed to collaborate with me on a book, for which he would send to our publisher the most arbitrary drawings which occurred to him, and it was I who christened the book with the only title appropriate to it: *Enigmas.*

I love and understand Dalí's mysteries, and I know as he should know that the water biscuits which we ate as children are food for the soul, for water biscuits are not just biscuits but significant events, like a hand stroking a dog's muzzle, the contact of the cold hand of death; that there are crepuscular objects like elephants made of ebony and that everything is mysterious except for the dead leaves which fall in the autumn.

Like him, I also believe in talismans.

Right now I have one of the utmost significance.

A little while ago I dreamed of a paperweight which had a kind of umbilical cord emerging from among the flowers and arabesques set into the glass, joining it to a strange and scrawny bird, so that one could not tell whether it was receiving life from or giving it to the paperweight's inextricable flora. On the very next day I saw in the windows of the Municipal Lending Bank a paperweight with a mushroom embedded in the mass of glass which seemed to bear some relation to my dream. I had never seen paperweights offered in a closed auction before, and had never made a sealed bid, but this time I did, and today I have it as a talisman, and it is bringing me luck.

Dalí's paintings are capable of various interpretations. His ants, for example, may represent the pleasure in excess which is a danger to health, an ant heap represents an excess of cerebration; but if one takes the significance they have in dreams, ants mean that one must look after one's joints.

Art is a new way of making extravagant statements, of

overcoming monotony by any means in an original and successful form.

We are producers of amusement for the rest, because the amusements which satisfied their ancestors are not enough for them.

Art is a running joke which is always taking new forms.

Find out what the current joke in art is and adopt it, or you will find yourself left behind.

Art is not a question of watching to see who is up to what.

It is very difficult to introduce the irrelevant, to jumble up the things of the apparent world, but the artist must be able to jumble them and unjumble them. In this way he can take the pulse of the absurd and give it reality.

Everything may seem possible to us in the art of the absurd, and yet this is not so, and if we make a mistake we shall lose our heads to the flaming angel of the inadmissible.

We must achieve a match between truth and unreality.

Anyone who wants to indulge in Dalíisms must be able to ask questions like "Can radar reach directly to Paradise?"

The associations of the Dalíist must be ultimately explicable, must be more than words like "exodental," which only have the meaning which one gives them, which in fact have no meaning at all.

Thus if we establish an association between a watering can and a watch, we must think of the drops of water as minutes coming out of the can, instead of rejecting any explanation and thereby tainting art with the label of vulgarity and the brutality of mere incomprehensibility.

This urge to materialize the images of concrete irrationality so that they would be as objectively apparent as the real phenomena of the exterior world was already to be found in baroque art, wherever it was not a dragon, a thistle, or a scroll which was materialized among the looming strata of its rocks.

Dalí aims to be—among many other things—an artist of the superbaroque, the superchurrigueresque, surpassing the rococo in complication, dragging out lichens and mysterious holes from the grotto of the irrational unconscious and flinging the Freudian lion in the face of the allegorical monster.

His asymmetrical windows, hard-boiled eggs, and niches with cameos far surpass the monotonous heraldic devices of armorial shields.

One must complicate simplicity and unravel complexity, see how one thing is transformed into another, how

forms change, how forms are formed—the morphosis of morphology.

What Dalí does should surprise no one, for it is no more than imagination, but it is "the germinal imagination of genius," and may God preserve us from the imagination of those who have no imagination.

One must be able to see the worlds created by others, above all when they are peaceful worlds, despite their strangeness. I can understand people reacting against worlds which threaten violence, the clean sweep of revolution, but not against imagined or imaginary worlds which add to the vitality of our culture.

Everyone tilts at Dalí, but what we need to do is to explain the polymorphism of this great and extraordinary painter.

Dalí has laid bare something of the unrevealed mystery of the world, even his revelations still at times being veiled.

Admittedly, he sometimes produces incomprehensible images, but let us not forget that a great philosopher once said that the incomprehensible is above intelligence while the unintelligible lies below it.

We must also realize that things without an external meaning still have a meaning of their own.

Dalí is a genius of the modern world, which means he is a genius of abuse.

Dalí decomposes and recomposes the world for us in the most extraordinary fashion, he is a past master of the macabre joke.

Speaking for the surrealists, he said: "Our ideal is to succeed in producing an art as pure as that of lunatics, but which is not that."

There is a hint of the bullfighter in him, for as he says, "I want to give the fierce *estocada* with which surrealism pierces the heart of reality."

Art is a matter of finding things which are expressive but have no relation to what has gone before.

Art is always something more, it is different and yet the same; it is based on our need to react against the monotony of the world, which is repetition.

With this in mind, Dalí presented himself as the naturally dissident Spaniard who changed his nature to become the dissident of dissidence, and it was he who uttered the famous cry "We must assassinate painting," a feat which he indeed accomplished, at least as far as a particular type of painting is concerned.

The one thing we must avoid is confusing his esthetics with his exhibitionist propaganda, which has been fed by phrases such as: "At the age of five I wanted to be a cock, at seven, Napoleon, and my ambition has grown constantly ever since."

At the beginning of his book *Sobre los secretos de la pintura (On the Secrets of Painting),* he has written: "The two most unfortunate things which can happen to a painter are firstly, to be a Spaniard, and secondly, to be called Dalí. Both of these misfortunes have happened to me."

When he is asked whether there are any people he admires, he replies: "Very few," and the list of those he does admire turns out to consist of his wife Gala, Einstein, Picasso, and himself.

When an interviewer asked him, "Of all the epithets which exist, which would you most like to be described by?" he replied: "Dalí, genius."

This riposte has earned him comparison with the great matador Guerra, who when asked which other bullfighters he believed in, said: "First me, then nobody . . . then anybody."

Even as a child he had a taste for extravagance and used to disguise himself as a king, and when he reached adolescence his costume became even more exaggerated, as he himself relates: "I wore sidewhiskers, long hair, a long bow tie, a waterproof cape which reached to the ground and which my parents had bought in a sale after the Great War. This was the period in which my manner of dress was at its most aggressive. Later, abandoning what seemed to me this highly romantic garb, I had my hair slicked down flat and wore wide 'Oxford' trousers of the kind which produce an extraordinary disturbance when one walks. It was because of these trousers that I was once chased across Madrid and took refuge in a tram on the advice of the police."

He also takes a delight in disguises and practical jokes, and he himself relates how he used to stroll round the family house: "Sometimes I took things to extremes, as when I used to walk along the paths surrounding my house in Port Lligat, carrying my arm in a sling, and on meeting my rowdy friends who were curious to know what had happened to my hand, I would put my finger to my lips and whisper, 'Shhh, it's asleep.' "

There was a period in which he went around dressed like a widower from one of his paintings, disguising the suggestion of a lunatic pageboy which otherwise marks his appearance.

Painters are easily startled and very sensitive to the menace of the present. They are highly conscious of scandal and quick to take fright.

They are easily triggered off, and any outside stimulus, however immediate or remote, sensitizes their canvases, sends them scrabbling about among their paints, keeps them on the alert, casting about, trying to transfer to canvas whatever they can feel around them. Dalí reacts most to anything which sparks off the creative fit, is a subject for a painting, a glimmer of colour, a vivid and representable phenomenon. Complexes, psychiatric problems, the grimace on the face of things, the supplicant hand—the hand of the artist—any of these things compels him to do a painting.

He has never favoured inspirational art, and a still life makes him flee in horror.

It is his nervousness, his artistic history, which has given excitement to his painting, always with a hint of the obsessive, something ghostly even when seen in the light of noonday, existing side by side with his passion and his penchant for painting the impossible.

He sallies forth bravely to confront phenomena, hallucinations, the relationship between grottoes and esplanades.

He is the scenographer of difficult situations, dangerous moments, improbable contrasts. His whole life is governed by the need to be receptive to the unexpected.

He accepts the theory of every new moment, paints the annunciation of every new season, synchronizes his palette with the time on the meridian of novelty.

Ever receptive, always coming home or going away, travelling, facing a constant demand for the outrageous comment, Dalí brings the unexpected, the unheard-of to painting.

Dalí is a scenographer in the theater of contemporary life, engaged in a constant quest for surprises; on his night table stands a portrait of his internal demon, the key to his dreams, the photograph of his personal destiny. He knows that the glory of an office consists in having many filing cabinets and drawers, a plethora of pigeonholes, and that in life we only have drawers—if we don't keep things in drawers then we have nothing. The pregnant woman, the musicians playing jazz, both partake of the ambiance of Dalí's night table.

He elevates the shoe—the fetishist's shoe—and turns it into a hat. Man is obsessed by shoes, which he sees as the ghosts of his feet.

Boots have suffered an eclipse at the hand of shoes. A massacre was ordered and they were cut off at the neck, turning them into shoes. But boots still live on, concurrently with shoes.

I cannot be less hypocritical than my fellow humans, so I will say sometimes shoes and sometimes boots, meaning the same thing.

Shoes mean more to man than one might think, for he sees them as the attendant spirits of his feet.

Shoes have always been important: a saint once threw a shoe into the heaving waves and calmed the storm, and it is still floating there now.

Shoes are the base of humanity, the common pedestal on which it stands.

What greater proof could there be that God sent man into the world as an extraordinary and privileged being than that he sent him barefoot and with sensitive soles, so that he could use his intelligence to invent shoes?

A tramp knows what shoes are worth, he knows the sensual delight of walking with them in his hand or over his shoulder as if they were made of lead or iron.

Thus there are men who appear to have been born wearing shoes, and others who seem to have been born in a state of shoeless poverty.

At dawn we see old men wearing lamentable broken shoes and we don't understand why someone cannot give them a used pair. Poor tramps walk slowly on their broken-down shoes because they have double rheumatism—in their feet and their shoes.

Shoes have personality, they can get tired on their own, and when our feet are hurting us we say: "My shoes are hurting."

Shoes can be a death mask of the toes—the big toe, the little toe—making us feel as though we have to cut our nails on the outside and not on the inside.

Dalí knows that there is a scatology of shoes, but there is also the simple psychology of shoes, which is what preoccupied poor Van Gogh. He was unable to get models—which is why he did so many self-portraits—and so painted potatoes and old, worn-out boots with ineffable sensitivity. These shoes—these boots of Van Gogh—which could not even buy him a cup of watery coffee, are now worth more than any pair of shoes, even shoes with the heels full of diamonds, for his painting *La Diligence de Tarascon* sold for $85,000.

Is Dalí, then, going to convert himself into the slave, the accomplice of reality, its latest disguise? Suddenly we find him painting, after Van Gogh and with a hundred

times his intensity, a pair of shoes which express all the desperation of human fatigue, all the wear and tear of old age. But at the same time he struggles victoriously against the baseness of reality and openly prescribes his own inoculation—the vaccine of love. Only a genius could think of placing next to that pair of shoes which have finally received the sentence of death the living, luminous foot, the triumphal grace of his goddess Gala. Its graceful buckle, deliciously bitten by the serpent of glory, emits an air of seduction which adds a saving grace to the humblest of humble footwear which it accompanies.

This token of poverty—Dalí does not believe in poverty—this suggestion of burial and resurrection which there is about old shoes, is always shocking, seeming to bear overtones of the communal grave.

There is a hierarchy of decay which begins when that fatal ulcer first appears in the heel, suggestive of a lymphatic adolescence, only to be followed by crow's feet, gaping sores, and finally gaping crocodile mouths; the patient's illness finally becomes evident as he lies down and dies.

Ask me what will remain of me when I am gone, and I will reply: "Very little . . . very little . . . There will be nothing left of me but a few old shoes, for that is all that remains of any worthy man, for all shoes lead finally to the same oblivion."

Dalí's art as a painter is his gift of imagining what the public wants, what will give it a shock and make it imagine that it is enjoying the future before it has happened.

It may recriminate and expostulate, but Dalí persists, changing and passing from surrealism to the Gothic.

Thus when Dalí, in New York, felt the first repercussions of the atomic bomb, he devoted part of his painting to prophesying the results of this monstrous phenomenon, producing fragmented lumps, boulders, capitals separated from their columns, like the debris of an atomic explosion.

Always something of a prophet, Dalí wanted to show things shattered and irradiated by the fusionary blast of this new phenomenon. Even his soft watches seemed to be drooping through the fear of a future atomic war.

In this portentous period, Dalí had himself photographed in his studio among flying cats, an exploding easel, himself flying up towards the ceiling. The trick photography must have been difficult and expensive, not to say violent, but Dalí managed to find some courageous photographer to carry it out.

A close study of this anxious painter of our anxious age

reveals that he was the first to take inspiration from the traumatic idea of an atomic explosion.

Another great painter, Leonardo, who lived in a time of perpetual wars and the beginnings of mechanical warfare, took time off from his painting, in all its serenity and magnificence, to invent engines of war.

Today Dalí's powers of invention cannot match this war of unlimited explosives and so he paints the psychology of its terror, of its juggernaut unstoppability.

On one of his arrivals in New York he declared that he had finished forever with "staticism" and would henceforth devote himself entirely to "dynamism," and that "explosion" would be the key to his new artistic thought.

His celebrated liquefying watch has been converted into a "watch exploding into 888 pieces," a number chosen by the artist after lengthy mathematical calculations and also as a "harmonic" number.

The explosions he is concerned with are "soft explosions," though still of the nuclear variety, which he sees as expressive of a kind of mysticism which runs counter to atomic conflagrations.

Where Dalí exceeds all bounds of taste and religious orthodoxy is in painting the Virgin as the victim of a nuclear blast, blown off her throne, the arch of her altar shattered, though the pieces still remain pacifically suspended in the air. Having begun with the "angel exploding harmonically," he continued with the Assumption of a Virgin shattered into lumps and disclike fragments like a puzzle; this he followed with the *Virgin of Port Lligat* and then an "explosive, nuclear, and hypercubic" Christ. The Christ is shown shattering into eighty pieces and is "the first painting whose conception is genuinely based on cubist elements unfolding in the fourth dimension."

Practically everything that Dalí has produced represents a working out of the dreams of his childhood and adolescence, is the result of a stubborn act of sublimation.

Thus the original orientation of his painting—since the initial period of naturalistic studies—is derived from his visits to the basement of the Prado museum on the days when he played truant from the school of San Fernando. The rooms in the basement contained a secret hoard consisting of all the strangest paintings in the museum's collection; it was an underworld, a kind of crypt of the pantheon of art, containing its most distinguished corpses and its most dazzling apparitions, among which were the works of that great painter El Bosco. In Spain we never said Hieronymus Bosch but always El Bosco, and the name seemed to hint at his sylvan interior world—something bosky and enchanted, dark and remote. El Bosco it was who rent the veil separating the Middle Ages from future periods, projecting a new light on his larval monsters and the anxieties which they symbolized. It was a remarkable performance, achieved without model or precedent.

El Bosco was the secret delight of those who thirsted for mysteries and divinations, and to him we went, eager for elucidation of the present world and the world beyond, of the world above and the world below; he was the perfect artist for a Spain living in a permanent dream, in the glory which precedes death and afterwards, hell.

Bosch was a unique and marvellous phenomenon of the late Middle Ages, for no critic has ever been able to explain how this artist hidden away in a remote hamlet set the whole of traditional painting on a new course, guiding it into dangerous and unfamiliar waters.

Elsewhere, in a few illuminated capitals, hiding their innovations in the embrace of the great initial letter, inside the paunch of the B or the sinuosity of the S, the miniaturists were already making their own contribution, letting themselves go, painting the singular, the outrageous, whatever sought freedom of expression.

Some religious artists, too, were active, in half-concealed panels on the other kind of capital, and in choir stalls—more beneath the sculpted seats than above, where serious figures reigned—taking advantage of these hidden locations to give sculptural expression to the siren, the fabulous monster, the couple of lovers giving way to furtive passion.

Then suddenly, El Bosco, facing the daylight in the window which gave onto the sixteenth century from the fifteenth, risked his all, still borrowing something from the miniaturists, only getting it past by dint of many distractions, but finally achieving the triumphal expression of his ideas.

The whole age was astounded, and the great inquisitors clamoured for his works, letting him name his price, among them no less a personage than Philip II, who bought his best paintings in the auctions at which they appeared.

The cataloguers of these works sometimes describe them as *disparates* (mistakes)—a word which was to find an echo in Goya, who solemnly chose it himself for part of his work—while Bosch called them "dreams."

This visionary of genius was well suited to the profoundly visionary Spain of the time, and his vibrant canvases illumined the interior of the Escorial. Philip II had the one entitled *The Cure for Madness* in his study, and as a night table for his spiritual medicines the round panel covered with thick glass entitled *Table of the Seven Deadly Sins,* in addition to which there were four more circular panels bearing allegories of the last stages of man — death, judgement, hell, and heaven.

The Earthly Paradise, which in a document consigning it to the monastery of El Escorial on July 8, 1503, is called "a painting of the variety of the world," is difficult to describe, a triptych pregnant with the anxiety of creation bearing down on man.

The great critic Carlos Justi says of this painting: "The most extraordinary of Bosch's allegorical moralizing creations is the one for which the correct title still remains to be found. The Spaniards call it *El Cuadro de la lujuria (The Painting of Lechery)* and also *Los Vicios y su fin (Vices and Their End).* The scene depicted appears to be a park full of wild vegetation, the rarest of flora and fauna; a kind of earthly paradise, judging also by the costume of its inhabitants. No doubt inspired by the news of the recent discovery of America, Bosch's imagination was in a ferment, overflowing with images of that tropical landscape.

"Here we see the same amazing trees and animals as in the other paintings of paradise. The proscenium of the left-hand panel, in which Eve, already formed, is presented to Adam, bears images of the great tropical species: the elephant, the giraffe, the kangaroo, and the unicorn which lived in countries known to the Middle Ages. Then, too, there are flying fish, birds with three heads, and gigantic dinosaurs. A marvellous vegetation proliferates in the background. A gigantic strawberry tree, the symbol of love, is growing on a hill. It is probably intended as a variety of the tree of knowledge.

"Some vegetable shapes, shoots from the same tree, numbering five in all, fill the background of the central panel. In front of them is a copse, a garden of Armida; a pool surrounded by undergrowth reflects a procession making its way slowly around it, men riding two or even three abreast, mounted on panthers, chargers, goats, bulls, lions, camels, bears, griffins, unicorns, hogs. Groups of nymphs playing in the water flirt with the riders. A witch on horseback is also to be seen in a celebration of naturalistic religion. At the front end the scene broadens out into the luxuriant and magnificent landscape of a

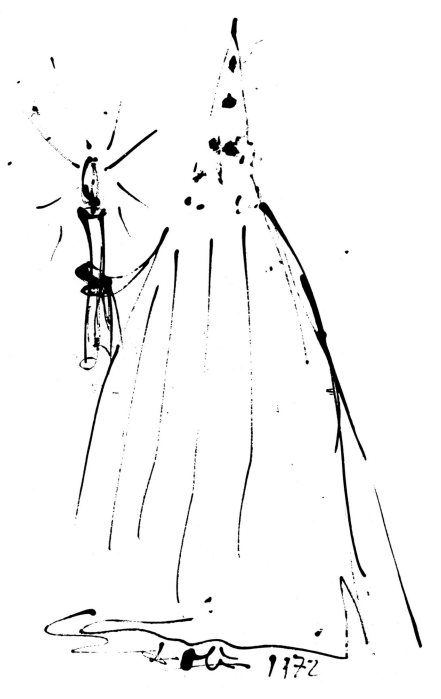

tropical swamp. Both flora and fauna are of colossal size. Innumerable groups are scattered across a landscape in which nature itself seems possessed by a taste for the marvellous, forming enchanted grottoes of vegetable forms. . . . Who could hope to follow all the twists and turns of the symbolic labyrinth which Bosch, the painter-moralist, has created here? Perhaps he intended the picture as an exposition of his encoded philosophy of sensuality, as a proclamation of those rights which were to be formulated by the Renaissance. Poets have always set the paradisiac pleasures of the senses in the bosom of an intoxicated nature. In the witch on horseback the painter is trying to show us how voluptuousness feeds on all the human passions (symbolized by the animals), and is derived from them in the first place. In *The Earthly Paradise* Bosch depicts the inexhaustible capacity which voluptuousness has for metamorphosis and adaptation.

"It is only a step from the Elysian Fields to Avernus and the cauldrons of sulfur, and the reader can no doubt guess what is represented by the right-hand panel of the triptych. The antithesis of this enchanted garden is hell—hell in all its blackness, but nevertheless illuminated by a bright light."

The Hay Wain, representing the carnal pleasures for which men kill each other—for, as the Bible says, "all flesh is grass"—is another of Bosch's major works. The one which most obviously brings us back to Dalí, however, is *The Temptations of St. Anthony*. Here Bosch rises to a superior intellectual level, since the medium of temptation is not lubricity but the absurd, as if the devil was trying to subvert the saint's soul through madness, having failed to do so through the temptations of the flesh.

The painting contains a hint of duality, the suggestion that it is the painter rather than the saint who has been tempted by pictorial apparitions, which forced him to paint them, and as Father Sigüenza says: "If we see strange things it is not his fault but ours."

It is here that the affinity with Dalí is most marked, the two artists being linked not only by the image of a soft, pink, erect squid, but also by the nature of the temptation, which in Dalí is however cruder and more in line with contemporary ideas.

Dalí is the "Freudian" painter of the sins of today, which are now called complexes, wish-fulfillment, schizophrenia, frustrations, etc.

Dalí has transferred his secret life to canvas with all its monsters, and he, as much as Bosch, deserves the definition of the Dutch painter given by Father Sigüenza: "The difference which there is, for me, between the paintings of this man and those of others, is that the rest only succeed in painting man as he is on the outside; only this man dares to paint him as he is on the inside."

The whole of the surrealist world sinned, but it had to be a Spaniard who showed the sin laid bare, blameless, repulsive.

The only thing lacking in Dalí's moral proclamation was the side of punishment, the section of the triptych showing hell, the purifying contrast; instead he painted the temptations again, this time more clearly, in a scatological spirit, with not an aberration spared.

Again, like Bosch, he mixes different levels of scenery, using the symbols of creation as the framework and background for his temptations. Rocks, esplanades, beaches, and in the middle the life of man, his writhings and his monstrosity shown out in the open, like beggars seated at the roadside displaying their sores.

The two painters both show a similar arrangement of the landscape, dotted with waves, using what Dalí himself called in the title of one of his paintings "enigmatic elements for a landscape."

Where Bosch paints dinosaur skeletons, Dalí uses skeletons of ships and fragments of the great egg beloved of both painters, while the two of them draw reptiles of unheard-of form.

Dalí's broken bridges are another source of static terror, for the drama of Dalí's work is that everything can turn into something else, be something else, split in the process of creation, suspend its normal outline, call on the magic of teratology.

As perception precedes action, so the revelation of Bosch's work nurtured a fondness for the extraordinary in Dalí, but in order to express it freely, he had to equip himself with "a prodigious technique and a lot of *tiento,*" the Spanish word being used both in the sense of caution and as the name of the maulstick which forms a major weapon in the painter's armoury.

The proverbial link of gold would be needed to join the chain which unites the imaginative and the real in "El Bosco" with the mystical and realist painter which is Dalí.

With his sudden damnations, his soul as accelerative as an intercity express, Dalí may be expected to revive the whole of biblical history, complete with Last Suppers, Miracles, and Martyrdoms.

That is how Dalí is—he passes from drunkenness to abstinence, from a sinner and blasphemer to a kneeling penitent, hammering his chest with his fists. He could

have painted things from the subconscious which were not sinful but angelic, and then he would not have had to renounce his discoveries and submit to the sadness of seeing the new forms lying stranded on the beach of renunciation, left for others to refloat.

A millennial weariness seems to have settled on the young rebel—the revealer of novelties, with his face of a man just returned from the spendthrift climate of the Philippines—as if he had been exhausted by his early adventures and were now content to live on the income from his dollars, painting serene replicas of museum pieces. Now there was not a hint of schism or heresy! In order to avoid it he illustrated *The Divine Comedy,* launched his works in gold and silver, and called a press conference to explain it all. "They were all there, even the Russian from the Tass agency, gathered with an escort of photographers under the streams of light from the 'Incom' newscaster, in the Loggia Pallavicini of the Palazzo Rospigliosi, with its ceiling fresco *La Auróra (The Dawn)* by Guido Reni, that sickening painter so beloved of Hegel and the other Romantics, who referred to him familiarly as 'Guido.' "

At the beginning there was great confusion. Dalí was busy arranging the mounting of his works, coming and going with his exotic cane crowned by a blue-and-orange duck's head. The famous jewels—the ruby mouth with pearl teeth, the *Archaic wound,* the *"Gold Heart with Coral Center"* which beat realistically, powered by an electric motor, and all the other jewels—were being set up on small urns covered in black velvet and bathed in indirect light. An American was solemnly explaining something with the air of the man in charge—he was a manager from the Catherwood Foundation of Pennsylvania, which not only commissions these works from Dalí but displays them all over the world "to promote the spiritual *rapprochement* of peoples." Some American reporters were asking the Spaniards, who seemed to be best informed: "What do you mean by a drawing of St. John of the Cross?"

Suddenly an enormous ladder fell on top of the *Assumption,* to the horror of workmen and reporters, but without causing any damage. In the central room pride of place was given to a white cube covered with letters, which was standing on a platform. Lying among the broken boxes left by the electricians was a piece of cardboard bearing a pencilled definition in Latin of the essence of this mysterious cube.

Cubus iste metafisicus quidem nove mee nativitas ovum

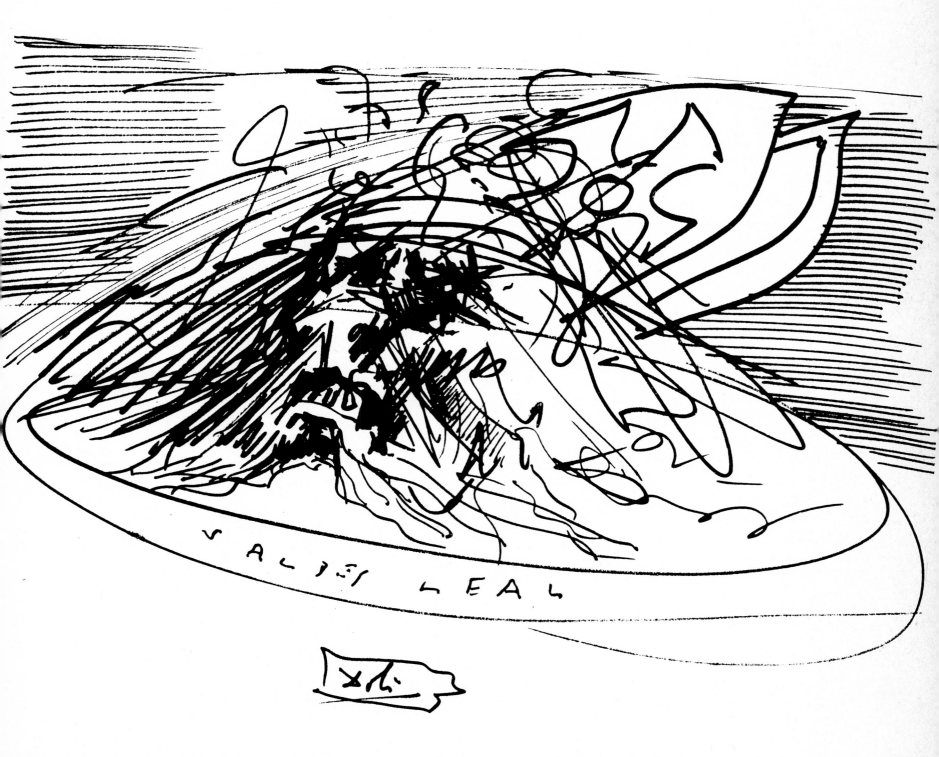

mes cubus iste revera esplendidisimus expicte exprimit simbolum opositum hidrogenico pirobolo. "The bit about *hidrogenico pirobolo* is the H-bomb," explained some journalist with a classical education, and went on to recall the Latin translation of *Pinocchio* for Italian children and the paper *Latinitas,* which contained accounts of football matches in the language of Virgil.

Suddenly the journalists were brought running from the other rooms: Dalí having mounted on top of the cube with the help of a fireman's ladder, erupted into action. Brandishing a microphone, he began to harangue the assembly in his Catalán-accented French, a duplicated resumé of his speech having been circulated beforehand.

Afterwards came the questions; inevitably, one of the subjects mentioned was Picasso:

"As a practicing Catholic I pray for Picasso every day. And I am prepared to make a prophesy: within twelve years—I myself am living twelve years behind everyone else—Picasso will have abandoned communism and will be producing religious paintings, because basically he is a mystic. I wrote him a letter: 'Cher Pablo: We are very grateful to you because you have freed us from so much ugly painting. The ugliness which the French began with Le Douanier Rousseau and would have taken years to produce, you have done for us in a moment.' "

The laughter which greeted this sally broke the ice and someone asked him why he wears his outlandish moustache.

"So as to pass unnoticed. Yes, I'll explain"—raising his voice above the laughter—"because while everyone is looking at the moustache I am doing what I want behind it."

Then he added something about its function as an antenna and smiled amiably at the questioner.

Suddenly things looked serious: Dalí was about to get the giggles.

Finally, he managed to contain himself, regained control, and passed on to another question. He made a rapid gesture, flipping open his outlandish waistcoat and raising something fleetingly to his lips.

"He kissed a medal," said a lady of religious inclinations. "No, it's licorice," suggested an ascetic-looking Spaniard.

Dalí then spoke courteously of Cézanne, and went on to relate how his wife Gala had been present at his birth, "at his first birth." Finally, amid a flurry of flashbulbs, he once more seized the fireman's ladder and jumped nimbly down from the cube, running to take up his position beside a painting for more photographs.

The little baroque garden at the entrance to the Loggia Pallavicini was still filled with late afternoon light. "These things ought to be done later in the day," complained a lady wearing a great deal of hat.

Dalí meanwhile was rejecting the supposition that the Spanish temperament, with all its nervousness and impatience, was not capable of such "excessively perfect" painting; one of his favourite anecdotes relates how when he took part in the entrance competition for the Academy of San Fernando, the canvas he produced was smaller than that prescribed by the rules, but it was so well done that this piece of miniaturization was excused.

Dalí is so original, his types of painting so new that even in times to come the body of his work in museums will constitute a reference to a world beyond, an expression of eternal themes, and this is surely the essence of the renewal of art.

If as Dalí has often said a new Middle Ages comes, the Middle Ages of some new age of majority, Dalí will be the painter of its dawning, as Hieronymus Bosch was of the sunset of the other.

Dalí's Virgin is original in that it is a levitating Virgin, and this levitation is extended to all the things which surround it, architecture and objects. For some time now, Dalí has been painting her as if she were the victim of an atomic explosion, disjointed, shot to pieces, floating in the air.

There is another original feature which distinguishes his Virgin from all the other Madonnas of the past: he has opened her chest like a casement, showing the sky which surrounds her in the background, and the Child Jesus is projected as if against a window on the entrailless, transparent torso of the Mother.

Like the juggler in the story by Anatole France, Dalí performs his juggling tricks in front of the Virgin as if hoping to earn her favour, and paints things of nature around her maternal bust like those painters who surrounded the central figure in their canvases with the things which they had brought back from their exotic journeys to the Indies.

God must have smiled on this new piece of painterly ingenuity, since his published list of sins includes neither the artistic sin nor the cubist sin.

On finishing his autobiography—the *Secret Life*—at

Filosofo materialista
comiendo un ZAPATO

1973

twelve noon on July 30, 1941, at Hampton Manor in the United States, Salvador Dalí, after fervently expressing his desire for God, wrote: "At this moment I do not yet have faith, and I fear I shall die without heaven."

Nevertheless, in various parts of his autobiography he was still aiming for the Vatican, and at one moment he said: "And if I am asked again today where the real force of Europe is to be found, I shall answer again that in spite of all immediate appearances it resides more than ever in the indivisibility of its spirit, in that indivisibility which is materialized in Bernini's two rows of columns, the open arms of the occident, the arms of St. Peter's in Rome, the cupola of man, the Vatican.

"As a citizen I consider the United Nations the highest authority and the one best qualified to discuss the atomic problem. And personally, I would wish that all the anti-materialists, without exception or distinction of beliefs, would listen with increasing fervour to the highest moral conscience of today.

"In my opinion, this is expressed by the Pope and the leaders who uphold spiritual and moral values in the face of the materialism and the violence of Marxist doctrine."

Dalí knows that without an ultimate mystical sense, the whole world has the quality of a rhinoceros.

Ten years had to pass, nevertheless, before Dalí, Catholically married to Gala after a love affair of seven years, went to Rome to see the Pope with his *Madonna of Port Lligat*, the Catalán beach on the Costa Brava where she first appeared to him.

As the Spanish critic José Maria Massip has said, "With this painting, Salvador Dalí appears to have found himself. I passed two long and agreeable winter afternoons talking to Dalí in the room of his Fifty-fifth Street hotel. One has the impression that his whole life is bound up in the charm of his Virgin.

"This summer he is going back to Cadaqués to paint her again on a much larger canvas than before, and he is proposing to exhibit her in New York next winter. He has prepared dozens of sketches and has planned the internal architecture of his canvas with an engineer's precision. The whole world of this painter—a painter who earns two thousand dollars a portrait and holds his clients to a strict rota—in the febrile, mechanized atmosphere of a luxury New York hotel, seems to have been filled with the blue landscape of Cadaqués.

"In the meantime, while the dust is settling around Dalí, the dust inevitably raised in any surroundings where Dalí is engaged in being himself, I thought that it could be interesting, as someone has suggested, to put a little order into the Dalí case, and it seemed to me that no one better than the man himself could help me, help all of us, in this considerable enterprise. I belong to the same generation as Salvador Dalí, I have known him and followed him for many years and there is one thing I have never doubted: his passionate sincerity, albeit a sincerity often obscured by the stories told about him and the truculence of his own personality."

The Pope, at any rate, with his great capacity for understanding, accepted the sincerity of the pilgrim painter's discourse.

Had Dalí's early work been less sinful no doubt he would have been required to go to Rome on his knees, but contrition is the most respectable of all human sentiments.

The first painter of the Atomic Age, on returning to his native shores, to the Catalonia which calls its cathedral La Sagrada Familia, bowed his head and was converted, once again becoming part of that great Catalán tradition of expressive religious painters who practice the sublimation of their own martyrdom.

In a lecture at the Ateneo Barcelonés, he explained his new mysticism, affirming that his present work is in the spiritual tradition of Zurbarán, Murillo, Valdés Leal, and the great mystics of literature, and concluded by reading a theological poem entitled "Atomic Perfection of the Annunciation of the Immaculate Conception."

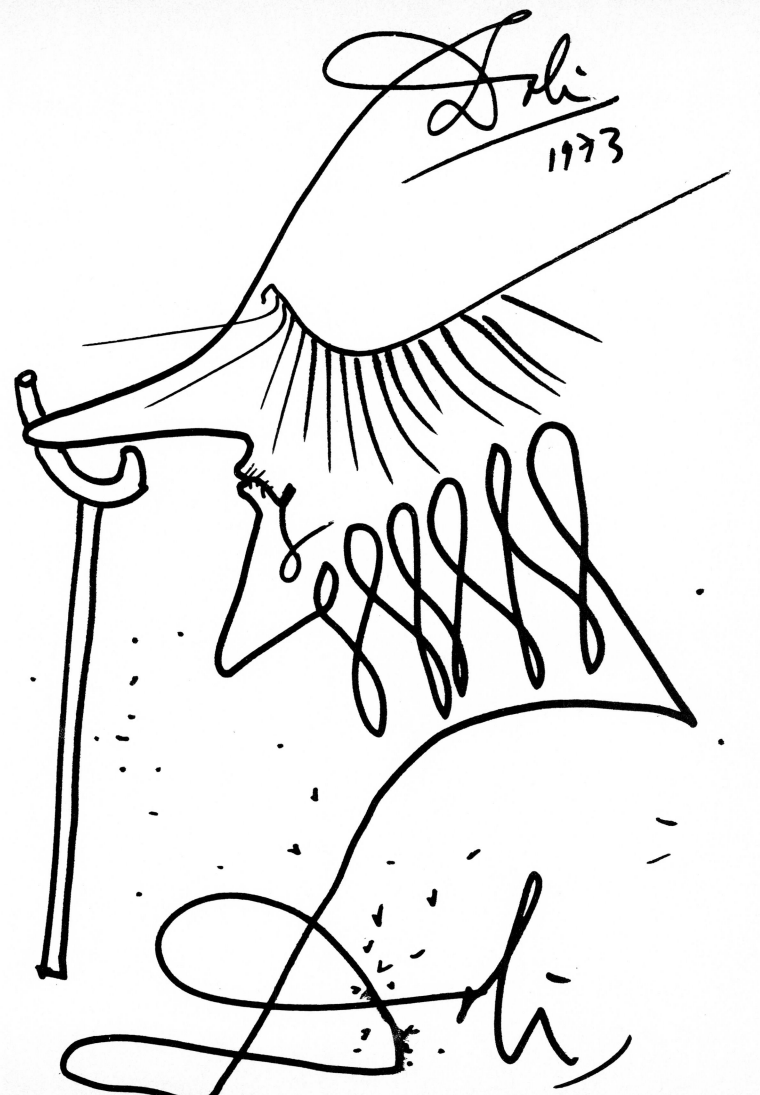

Ramón Gómez de la Serna and Dalí

Note by Sebastiano Grasso

When on January 12, 1963, death stilled the hand of Ramón Gómez de la Serna in Buenos Aires, he was working on a critical biography—of sorts—on Salvador Dalí. The two Spaniards had agreed that Dalí would illustrate the text.

About fifteen years passed before the book was actually published. The manuscript was among the papers of Gómez de la Serna that passed to his heir Eduardo G. Ghioldi. It was incomplete, but extremely interesting.

Dalí respected Ramón's wishes and did the illustrations. They had not been particularly close friends, but they had admired each other's work. The interview with Dalí that completes the book quotes him as saying, "Gómez de la Serna did not know me personally very well. But even so there are three or four insights about my painting in it which no one else has had. And that is fundamental. If he had lived, Gómez de la Serna would have ended up a metaphysical monarch like me, and then indeed his book about me would have had no equal."

Ramón's portrait is of Dalí's moods, ideas, and ways of realizing them. He writes with obvious enjoyment. He was a writer used to "joking with Spain." Correa Calderón described him: "At first sight he looked a bit of a clown; an illusionist dressed up as a peasant. His black-and-white checked cravat looked like a sort of cigarette packet and he carried a slim, aristocratic cane that belonged to Larra."

He still managed to catch the most unusual aspects of Dalí's character, but only in flashes of inspiration. Life was a staircase which Ramón climbed, occasionally pretending to fall down a few steps to keep the spectator worried. From the top he dropped down a red handkerchief full of musical notes that turned into *greguerías* as they touched the ground. They have been described by Orio Vergani as "fragmentary notes of lyrical and ironic realities, somersaulting images, radioscopic examinations of sensations, collections on a highly musical pentagram of a prose as gilded and precise as enamel."

For Ramón scandal became entertainment, and like a true satirist making a pretence at self-pity he attracted the displeasure of the entire Barcelona Academy, scandalized by Dalí's work. But, Ramón admits, "it is a lonely walk into the future."

Who does Ramón Gómez de la Serna think Dalí is? Just "the offspring of a new species" who needs defending. So defense counsel Ramón makes a long, convincing, human, witty, and original speech in his defense.

Lots of people accuse the painter of madness. Dalí replies: "The only difference between me and a madman is that I am not mad." Ramón adds that at the very most Dalí tried to imitate madness in a "paranoiac-critical" age, since the Catalán artist was "a lonely adolescent who stayed an adolescent," defined by Freud as "a great Spanish fanatic."

Ramón followed Dalí step by step in his metamorphosis. He even participated in the operation and took a

Opposite page:
Ramón Gómez de la
Serna at thirty.
Left: Ramón Gómez
de la Serna interviews
a wax model in the
tower in calle
Velázquez. Dalí
invented
"hyperrealist"
anagrams of his
friend's name:

Gamez de la Selia,
Jermes de la Sernia,
Goser de la Sierre,
Gregez de la Seria,
Sernia de la Gregia.

certain pleasure in identifying with the artist. Dalí's extravagances become "seraphic" behaviour. The story develops. He comes to surrealism. Ramón had already described its "definition and doctrine" in the *Ismos,* so here limits himself to describing a succession of quick insights into what happened. His attention moves to Paris (described as a "wild beast returning with her new hovels and other tricks"), the home of poets and artists at a time when everything was brought into question. Even an "exhibition of lepers from Madagascar with vitamins doled out to students and watercolours painted by the obese" was possible.

The era of surrealism. Dalí triumphed in New York and Breton insultingly awarded him the anagram title Avida Dollars. Someone cries out: "Dalí has become commercialized." Ramón retorts that "the salesmen are Dalified."

So the inventor of the *greguerías* throws himself headfirst into surrealism, passing on to existentialism, which he dismisses as merely giving the illusion of novelty. So he turns to Dalí and defines him as a "truly innovative artist," the "scenographer of difficult things," who "dared what other men did not do in painting" (and did not Ramón himself achieve the same for writing?), the "Freudian painter of new sins known as complexes, split personality, unsatisfied dreams, etc.," a mystic and realist like Bosch (called El Bosco in Spanish), both imaginary and real.

The only neo Ramón can find in Dalí is that there is no *h* in his name.

"Thus the original orientation of his painting," says Ramón, "—since the initial period of naturalistic studies— is derived from his visits to the basement of the Prado museum on the days when he played truant from the school of San Fernando."

This is a biographical detail. After it Ramón sets out to plumb the secret depths of the painters whose works were in the basement of the Prado. Especially Bosch, whom he compares with Dalí's "damnations."

The long tale ends with a section on the Virgin of the Catalán artist in relation to the atomic bomb, that has something original "in that it is a levitating Virgin, and this levitation is extended to all the things which surround it, architecture and objects. For some time now, Dalí has been painting her as if she were the victim of an atomic explosion, disjointed, shot to pieces, floating in the air. . . . Like the juggler in the story by Anatole France, Dalí performs his juggling tricks in front of the Virgin as if hoping to earn her favour."

The structure of the essay on Dalí is borne out by Ramón's other biographies. Biography in itself is a mixture of erudition, intuition, and interpretation, and the wholehearted participation of the biographer is needed.

How to approach Ramón's biographical methods? He does not give his work a chronological structure. In *Effigies* he expresses some of his theories on biography and the biographer. The biographer, he says, must also be an historian. It does not matter if the "product" has an anach-

Banquet in honour of Ramón Gómez de la Serna at the Lhardy Restaurant in Madrid. Second from the left in front of the table is Federico García Lorca.

ronistic character. Quite the contrary. *Conditio sine qua non,* the vivacity, rhythm of the word, imaginative invention. Evocation must not become solemnization. Ramón brings a character to life. He creates imaginary situations for them and invents impressions and developments.

Torrente Ballester wrote, "The whole of Ramón's biographical work is an enlarged *greguería.* First, he chooses to write about artists and writers whose lives or art deviates from the norm . . . which leaves him free to penetrate and discover the key to the mystery of authors' lives."

So there is a sort of osmosis between Ramón and his characters.

Why did Ramón write so many biographies? After he had finished about a hundred books in the '30s, when he was at his prime he began something different. From the analysis of a few authors he turned to the whole European spectrum of the arts and literature.

Why this enthusiasm? According to Luis S. Granjel in his book *Retrato de Ramón,* it is "his age, which allows him to remember, without nostalgia, his past, and even the lives and ideals of certain men and times. The second reason was the increasing demand in the '30s by the ordinary reader for biographies and books about recent events." It was what publishers wanted and Ramón took up the challenge because he wanted "to live by the pen." But he felt bitter about having to be a biographer. In a letter to Granjel he confessed: "I'm desperate at having to write so many biographies; you lose your own identity thinking about others in the past and present."

As it was, besides being a "juggler with words," Ramón became "the attentive chronicler of Spanish literary life of the '20s." Studies, notes, *greguerías.* He wrote a great deal. "The publishers don't manage to keep up with me," he said. Orio Vergani called him "a valiant man working in the service of literature . . . patient as a Chinaman, prolific as a Latin, methodical as a German."

In copies of *Ismos,* considered by Spanish readers "the first and best publication about European avant-garde art and literature," Ramón wrote about many leading figures such as Toulouse-Lautrec, Archipenko, Lipchitz, Lhote, Delaunay, Léger, Laurencin, Rivera, Chagall, de Falla, Swinburne, Fort, Gourmont, Lorrain, Roux, Wilde, Baudelaire, de Nerval, Ducasse, Eluard, Apollinaire, Cassou, Maeterlinck, Ehrenburg, Ibsen, Shaw, Kafka, Neruda, d'Annunzio, Pirandello, Bontempelli, Pitigrilli, and Marinetti (and defended futurism in *Prometeo).*

Later, between 1959 and 1961, his biographies were collected together into *Biografías completas* (El Greco, Goya, Velázquez, Gutiérrez-Solana, Lope de Vega, Quevedo, Edgar Allan Poe, Coronado, Azorin, Valle-Inclán), and in *Retratos completos* (containing *Effigies,* the *Retratos Contemporáneos,* part of *Ismos,* and other studies). These were generally monographs on art movements or paintings (as early as 1908 and 1910 Ramón contributed articles on art to the magazine *Prometeo,* and his first article on Picasso was in the *Revista de Occident).*

However, for Ramón biography remained the "best interpretation of the soul and of the author." He said, "My biographies are special. I dwell on what I consider essential and ignore the rest. . . . In biographies only a sigh, a cry, a quick glance or brief unconnected incident and whirlwind encounter should be included."

In his portrait of Edgar Allan Poe he wrote, "I am convinced that biography is something a biographer may or may not deserve to do. If he deserves it, the book will turn out right, if not all his efforts are in vain." This is why he preferred to take no risks, and as it concerned him wrote *Automoribundia.*

To one who lived exclusively to write, life is only a part of literature and death is a page torn out in anger.

A corner in Ramón's study reconstructed by the city of Madrid in the Casa de la Panadería, now in the Museo Municipal.

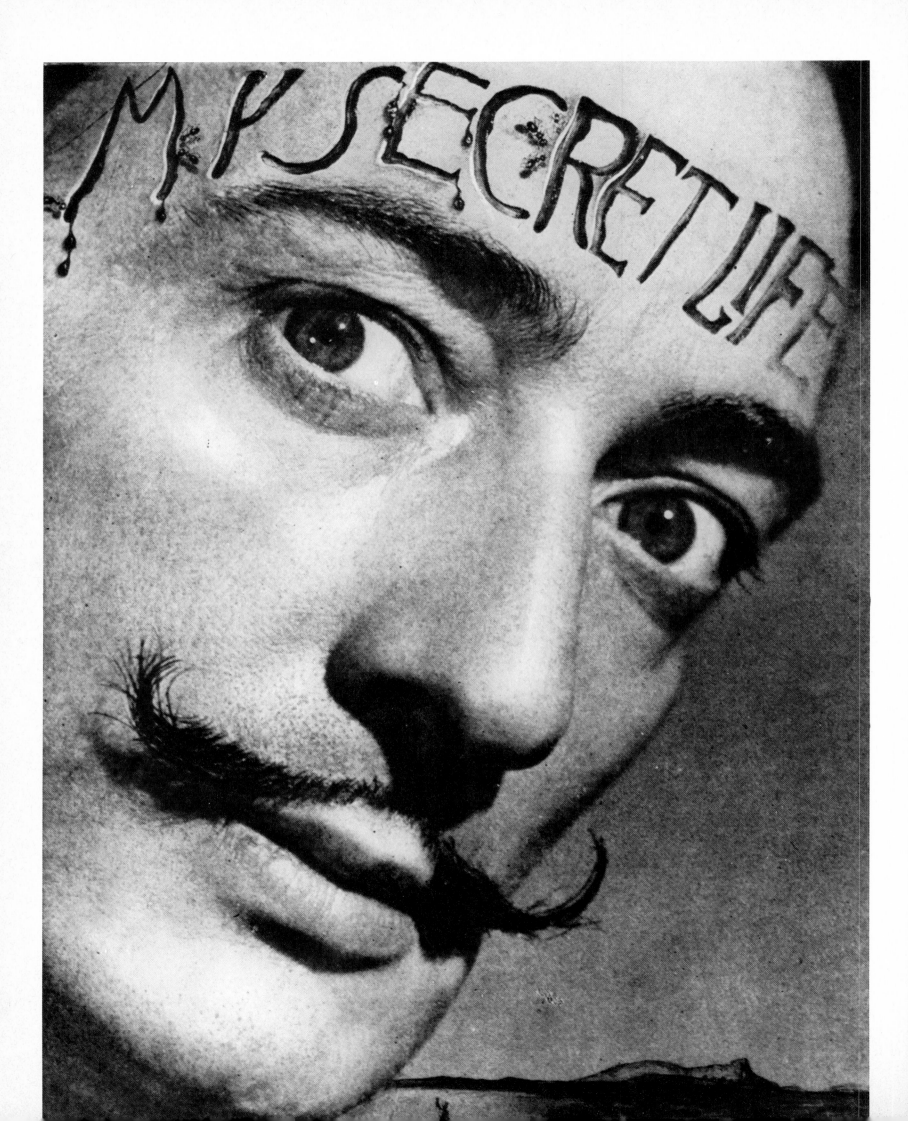

The Life and Works

Chronology by Eleonora Bairati

1904

Salvador Felipe Jacinto Dalí born on May 11 at Figueras, a little town on the Ampurdán plain in northern Catalonia, to Don Salvador Dalí y Cusí, notary, and Felipa Domenech.

Dalí felt a close bond for his birthplace and for Catalonia which marked his art, his way of life and his character from earliest childhood. He wrote, "At six I wanted to be a chef. At seven Napoleon."

1914-18

Dalí completed his secondary schooling at Figueras and showed an early interest in painting and the figurative arts, as well as creative activity of every kind, and developed into an unusual and extravagant character. He took private lessons in painting from the artist Nuñes, professor at the Academy of Art.

A rapid succession of events built the foundations of the postwar avant-garde movement in the aftermath of the destruction that had shaken Europe. Marcel Duchamp created his first "ready-made" (1913–15) and the Italian futurists made exciting and original experiments (from 1915). Prampolini and Depero were at work on their plastic polymaterial structures from 1915. Metaphysical painting was launched by Giorgio de Chirico and Carlo Carrà (1916–18) and in 1916 experiments made by the "Cabaret Voltaire" in Zurich gave birth to Dada, with its first manifesto written by Tristan Tzara in 1918. These were all important influences on Dalí as he formulated his own artistic creed.

1916-19

Dalí's first paintings show the clear influence of Spanish artists such as Modesto Urgel, Ramón Pichot, and Mariano Fortuny, but also an understanding of the historical background of modern painting, the impressionists and the French neo-impressionists.

He paints *Aunt Ana Sewing in Cadaqués* (1916–17); Joaquín Vila-Moners collection, Figueras; *Crepuscular Old Man* (1918–19); Ramón Pichot collection, Barcelona.

1919

Dalí's first articles and illustrations published in the magazine *Stadium,* published in Figueras.

The Catalán painter Joan Miró goes to Paris. He is to become a friend of Dalí and leading light of surrealism. Marcel Duchamp causes a scandal with his retouched "ready-made," the famous *Mona Lisa with a Beard.*

Bauhaus founded at Weimar. It was to be a hotbed of ideas about architecture and the visual arts linked to the abstract and structural currents in the European avant-garde movement (with very close links with the Dutch movement of De Stijl and his mentor Piet Mondrian, and Russian constructivism). Dalí always refuted the value of abstract art in his painting and writing.

1920-21

Admitted to the San Fernando Institute, the fine arts school of Madrid, where he studies drawing, painting, and sculpture and comes into close contact with the avant-garde movement, especially by studying Cézanne and Italian futurism (these clearly influenced his work at this time, especially the portraits, landscapes, and still lifes); in Madrid he comes into contact with literary and artistic circles and meets Luis Buñuel and Federico García Lorca. Dada at its height in Paris and the future protagonists of surrealism play a part in it: André Breton, Max Ernst, Hans Arp, Francis Picabia.

He paints *Self-portrait,* 1920–22, Salvador Dalí Foundation, Inc., St. Petersburg, Florida; *Self-portrait,* 1921, Gala-Dalí; *Portrait of My Father,* 1921, Gala-Dalí; *Cadaqués Seen from Inland,* 1921, private collection.

1922

He works mostly at Cadaqués, a village 28 km from

Figueras, the birthplace of his father, who had a country house there, and as Dalí loved the place he always had a studio there. In October he exhibits eight paintings at a collective exhibition of the Madrid Academy of Art at the Galería Dalmau in Barcelona.

He paints *Still Life with Fruit,* private collection; *Cadaqués,* Montserrat Dalí Collection, Barcelona; *Self-portrait with Neck of Raphael,* 1922–23, private collection, Paris; *The First Days of Spring,* 1922–23, Ramón Estalella Collection, Madrid.

In Paris André Breton becomes editor of the review *Littérature,* the basis of surrealism, at that time only involving three artists, Francis Picabia, Max Ernst, and Man Ray.

1923

Dalí suspended from the academy for insubordination against the academic authorities and for some of his more outlandish ideas. He is thoroughly assimilating the formal techniques and values of avant-garde painting through the work of Juan Gris and the Italian metaphysicians (de Chirico).

His most important painting is *Muchachas,* Teatro Museo Dalí, Figueras. In Spain the military dictatorship of General Primo de Rivera established.

1924

Dalí spends a short time in prison in Figueras and Gerona—apparently for political reasons, as he was suspected of anarchism.

Illustrations for *Les Bruixes de Llers* by C. Fages de Climent mark the beginning of one of Dalí's greatest periods as an artist.

He paints *Purist Still Life* (Teatro Museo Dalí, Figueras).

In Paris André Breton publishes the *First Surrealist Manifesto* and founds the magazine *La Révolution surréaliste.*

1925

Readmitted to the Academy of Art, Dalí is finally expelled in 1926; in November he has his first one-man exhibition (seventeen paintings and five drawings) at the Galería Dalmau in Barcelona, an avant-garde gallery that had previously shown work by Picabia in 1922, and from the end of the year collaborates with the Barcelona *Gaceta de Arte,* which continues until 1929.

Dalí is by now well known among young Catalán artists. Picasso sees his exhibition in Barcelona and expresses an interest in him.

He paints *Port Alguer,* private collection; *Girl Seen from Behind,* Museo Español de Arte Contemporáneo, Madrid; *Girl Seen from Behind Looking Out of the Window,* Museo Español de Arte Contemporáneo, Madrid.

Dalí wrote of the *Girl Seen from Behind:* "While I was painting it I had the shattering vision of a terrifying rectangular opening in her back."

First surrealist exhibition in Paris at the Galerie Pierre, with works by Arp, de Chirico, Ernst, Miró, and presented by Breton and Rorbert Desnos. Louis Aragon visits Madrid and holds a conference on surrealist ideas: links between the French and Spanish surrealist movements are strengthened, especially due to Spanish artists such as Miró and Picasso himself.

1926

Dalí starts to contribute regularly to the periodical *L'Ami des arts (Gaceta de Sitges)* until 1929. He seeks publicity either to defend and explain his art or later as an open-minded way of managing himself and attracting attention. Joan Miró visits him in Figueras with the dealer Pierre Loeb; an important encounter as Miró acts as intermediary between Dalí and surrealism. At the end of the year he has his second one-man exhibition at the Galería Dalmau in Barcelona (twenty paintings and seven drawings).

He paints *Basket of Bread,* Salvador Dalí Foundation, Inc., St. Petersburg, Florida; *Figure of a Woman,* circa 1926, Teatro Museo Dalí, Figueras.

The great Catalán architect Antonio Gaudí dies in Barcelona; his extraordinarily metamorphic and imaginative work was in its own way "surrealist" and always fascinated Dalí, who was directly inspired by them.

Federico García Lorca writes his *Ode to Salvador Dalí:*

> *O Salvador Dalí of the olive-tinted voice*
> *I speak of the things your person and your paintings*
> * tell me.*
> *I do not sing praises to your imperfect adolescent*
> * paintbrush,*
> *But I laud the firm direction of your arrows.*
>
> *I sing of your beautiful struggle of Catalán lights,*
> *Of your love of what is explained.*
> *I sing of your great tender heart,*
> *From French writings, and with no injury.*

André Breton opens the Galerie Surréaliste in rue J. Callot, Paris.

1927

Visits Paris for one week with his aunt and sister and meets Picasso for the first time. The two most famous Spanish artists of the century were different in art and temperament and never became friends.

Dalí remembered his meeting with Picasso, when at the doorway they stopped and looked at each other as if to say, "Do you understand? Yes, you understand."

Paints *Apparatus and Hand,* Salvador Dalí Foundation, Inc., St. Petersburg, Florida; *Self-portrait Splitting into Three,* Teatro Museo Dalí, Figueras; *Woman's Head,* Teatro Museo Dalí, Figueras.

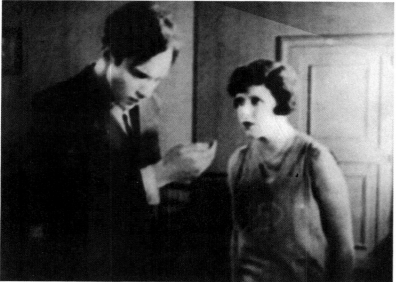

His work at this time is influenced by the cubist breakdown of form and the abstract surrealism of Hans Arp. Louis Aragon, André Breton and Paul Eluard join the French Communist Party: this was regarded by the party with suspicion and their membership was short and stormy, but surrealist "revolutionary" zeal continues to inspire comment.

1928

Dalí goes to Paris on the advice and invitation of Miró, who introduces him to other surrealists, such as Breton and Paul Eluard. Dalí sees the surrealist experiments of Yves Tanguy, René Magritte, and Max Ernst. Publishes the *Groc Manifesto* at Sitges in Spain, with Sebastian Gasch and Lluis Montanya. Three of his works are shown at the International Exhibition of Painting at the Carnegie Institute in Pittsburgh—the first contact the American public has with Dalí's work. At the end of the year he makes the film *Un Chien andalou* with his friend Luis Buñuel, one of the most amazing works of avant-garde cinema.

Already Dalí's work shows a very deep understanding of surrealist ideals expressed in original forms, in spite of its close connection with Tanguy and Ernst.

He paints *Anthropomorphic Beach,* polymaterial collage, Salvador Dalí Foundation, Inc., St. Petersburg, Florida; *Putrefied Birds,* circa 1928, Teatro Museo Dalí, Figueras; *Torso,* circa 1928, Teatro Museo Dalí, Figueras; *Nude Torso,* circa 1928, Teatro Museo Dalí, Figueras; *Inaugural Gooseflesh,* Ramón Pichot collection, Barcelona.

André Breton publishes in Paris his article on *Le Surréalisme et la peinture.*

1929

Dalí officially joins the surrealist group. During the summer the writer René Char and the poet Paul Eluard and his wife Elena (Gala) visit Dalí at Cadaqués; it is love at first sight between the artist and the twenty-five-year-old Gala, known as "the surrealist muse." From then on she is his faithful companion and a constant inspiration to his life and work. Their honeymoon is two days before the opening of Dalí's first one-man exhibition (eleven paintings) at the Galerie Goëmans in Paris, presented by Breton. At the end of the year the showing of *Un Chien andalou* at Studio 28 in Paris causes scandal and sensation.

He paints *Ghosts of Two Automobiles,* circa 1929, Teatro Museo Dalí, Figueras; *Portrait of Paul Eluard,* Gala-Dalí; *The Accommodation of Desire,* Julien Levy collection, Bridgewater, Connecticut; *Illuminated pleasures,* Mr. and Mrs. Janis collection, Museum of Modern Art, New York; *The Great Masturbator,* private collection; *Lugubrious Game,* C. H. Hersaint Collection, Paris.

He declares: "Gala is trinity. She is Gradiva, the woman who advances. And, according to Paul Eluard, she is a woman who can see through solid walls."

On page 54: Dalí by Dalí, for the cover of his autobiography, published in New York in 1942 under the title The Secret Life of Salvador Dalí. *On this page: two frames from Buñuel and Dalí's film* Un Chien andalou.

He writes about *Un Chien andalou*: "The film had the effect I promised myself: in one evening it ruined ten years of falsely intellectual postwar avant-garde. That indecent thing, abstract art, collapsed mortally wounded at our feet. There was no more room in Europe for M. Mondrian's maniacal little lozenges."

The final number of *La Révolution surréaliste* comes out containing the Second Surrealist Manifesto by Breton, illustrated by Dalí.

1930

Gala's tact and prudence constantly maintained a balance between Dalí and the surrealist group; he begins working for the periodical *Le Surréalisme au service de la Révolution* and publishes a collection of essays and poems called *La Femme visible* dedicated to Gala at the Editions Surréalistes; his poem "The Great Masturbator," named after the painting of the same name of the previous year, gives a foretaste of his theories of painting as a psychoanalytical and dialectic method. He illustrates *L'Immaculée Conception* by Breton and Eluard. Makes the film *L'Age d'or*, again in cooperation with Buñuel. While at Studio 28 in Paris for a few days he provokes violent protest from the right-wing League of Patriots organization (works by Ernst, Dalí, Ray, Tanguy and Miró exhibited in the theater club were destroyed), who had Buñuel's film banned as "Bolshevik." This episode causes a break in Dalí's friendship with Buñuel, and Dalí disassociates himself from the surrealists' political commitment.

He begins reflecting on the double image by studying Böcklin and Vermeer and embarks on an extraordinary return to the sources of European art which continually inspired his work.

He paints *Vertigo* (Carlo Ponti collection, Rome).

He writes: "Since 1929 I have reacted against the 'total revolution' unleashed by the anxieties of those who dabbled in the postwar phenomenon. Throwing myself with the same enthusiasm as they into the most subversive and mad speculations, I now began to prepare, with the Machiavellian cunning of a skeptic, the structural basis of the next historical rung on the way to eternal tradition."

Fall of the dictator Primo de Rivera in Spain.

A new periodical comes out in Paris, *Le Surréalisme au service de la Révolution,* that lasts until 1933.

1931

Exhibits seven paintings and two drawings at the Newer Super-Realism Exhibition at the Wadsworth Atheneum at Hartford, Connecticut.

Gala and Dalí buy the fisherman's cottage at Port

Scenes from L'Age d'or, *the film by Buñuel and Dalí.*

Lligat, a little way from Cadaqués, that is to become their home.

He writes *L'Amour and la mémoire* for the Editions Surréaliste and edits the general catalogue of surrealist objects (in *Le Surréalisme au service de la Révolution*), in which he champions "decadent, civilized, and European Art Nouveau objects" over the "wild objects" venerated by the avant-garde.

He paints *The Persistence of Memory (Soft Clocks)*, Museum of Modern Art, New York; *Six Apparitions of Lenin on a Piano*, Musée Nationale d'Art Moderne, Paris; *Old Age of William Tell*, private collection, Paris; *Portrait of Gala*, Albert Field collection, New York.

He declares ". . . the surrealist object, the irrational object with a symbolic function, against the contents of dreams and automatic writing."

Big revival of Catalán modernism and the work of Antonio Gaudí. Dalí declares: "The *Sagrada Familia* is the first manifestation of Mediterranean Gothic. The sublime Gaudí, who was an adolescent travelled to Cabo Creus, was fed on the soft baroque rocks, the hard and geometric rocks of this divine place."

In Spain the Constitution is reinstated; in April the Republicans win the elections; in December Catalonia is declared autonomous.

1932

Three paintings, including the *Persistence of Memory*, exhibited at the Julien Levy Gallery in New York—the beginning of Dalí's enormous success in America.

He writes *Babaou* (Editions des Cahiers Libres, Paris), with critical essays on the cinema and an essay on the story of William Tell.

He illustrates *Le Revolver à cheveux blancs* by Breton. He paints *The Birth of Liquid Desires*, Peggy Guggenheim collection, Venice; *Medium, Fine, and Invisible Harp*, private collection, Paris; *Portrait of the Vicomtesse de Noailles*, private collection in Paris; *Oeuf sur le plat sans le plat*, Salvador Dalí Foundation, Inc., St. Petersburg, Florida.

1933

First one-man exhibition in New York at the Julien Levy Gallery. Takes part in Paris in the collective exhibition "Le Surréalisme en 1933" at the Galerie Pierre Colle; in December his surrealist works are exhibited for the first time in Spain at the Galería Catalonia in Barcelona. He contributes to the surrealist review *Minotaur*, which comes out for the first time in 1933 and continues until 1937, and this includes his first reflections on Millet's *Angelus*. His work of this time obsessively repeats the theme of the brain and cephalic deformations.

He paints *Soft Clocks*, Luciano Pistoi Collection, Turin; *The Invisible Man*, Gala-Dalí; *Average Atmospher-*

ocephalic Bureaucrat in the Act of Milking a Cranial Harp, Salvador Dalí Foundation, Inc., St. Petersburg, Florida.

He writes: "The *Angelus* of Millet, as beautiful as the chance encounter, on a dissecting table, of a sewing machine and an umbrella."

1934

The increasingly apparent differences between Dalí and the surrealists, particularly Aragon, because of his political beliefs, causes Breton to decree that he should be expelled from the group after a sort of trial which Dalí tries hard to turn into a farce. However, this has no effect on Dalí whose international reputation is already established. He holds his first one-man exhibition in England (sixteen paintings, twenty drawings, and seventeen sketches) at the Zwemmer Gallery in London and makes a first visit to New York under the patronage of an admirer, Caresse Crosby; he starts to collaborate with the *Cahiers d'art.*

He makes forty-two sketches illustrating *Les Chants de Maldoror* by the Comte de Lautréamont (pseudonym of Isidore-Lucien Ducasse), a favourite text for the surrealists. A series of his illustrations of New York appear from February to July in the *American Weekly* review.

He paints *The Specter of Sex Appeal,* Teatro Museo Dalí, Figueras; *Atavistic Remain After the Rain,* Galerie F. Petit, Paris; *The Weaning of the Furniture-Food,* Salvador Dalí Foundation, Inc., St. Petersburg, Florida; *Atmospheric Skull Sodomizing a Grand Piano,* Salvador Dalí Foundation, Inc., St. Petersburg, Florida; *The Ghost of Vermeer of Delft which can be Used as a Table,* Salvador Dalí Foundation, Inc., St. Petersburg, Florida.

Elections in Catalonia bring in a left-wing government.

1935

He takes part in a surrealist exhibition held in Tenerife, Canary Islands, and patronized by the periodical *Gaceta de Arte* and by the local artist Oscar Dominguez—one of the most extraordinary episodes in the history of surrealism in Spain.

He illustrates *Grains et issues* by Tristan Tzara for the Editions Surréalistes and writes *The Conquest of the Irrational,* Editions Surréalistes, Paris, and Julien Levy, New York, his first important theoretical writing, which attracts the attention of a young and as yet unknown psychiatrist, Jacques Lacan, who analyzes its origins.

He paints the *Angelus of Gala,* J. D. Rockefeller, Jr., Collection, Museum of Modern Art, New York.

He defines "the paranoiac-critical method of irrational knowledge based on the critical interpretive association of delirious phenomena."

1936

Participates in the Exposition Surréaliste d'Objets at the Galerie Ratton in Paris and writes an essay entitled *Honneur à l'objet,* in the special number of *Cahiers d'art.* Dalí's first stay in America consolidates his fame; for the first time he meets the English collector Edward F. W. James, who patronized Dalí until 1938, commissioning many works (including *Suburbs of a Paranoiac-critical City,* and *Afternoon on the Borders of European History,* among the most important of the surrealist period.

He paints *The Great Paranoiac,* Edward F. W. James Collection, Tate Gallery, London; *Couple with Clouds Around Their Heads,* Edward F. W. James Collection, Tate Gallery, London; *Venus de Milo with Caskets,* gesso sculpture, private collection, Paris; *The Chemist of Figueras Who Is Looking for Absolutely Nothing,* Edward F. W. James collection, Sussex, England; *Geological Justice,* Edward F. W. James collection, Sussex, England; *Solar Table,* Edward F. W. James Foundation, Brighton Art Gallery, Brighton; *Perspective,* E. Hoffmann Foundation, Kunstmuseum, Basel; *Three Young Surrealist Women Holding in their Arms the Skins of an Orchestra,* Salvador Dalí Foundation, Inc., St. Petersburg, Florida; *Soft Construction with Cooked Beans—Premonition of Civil War,* Louise and Walter Arensberg collection, Philadelphia Museum of Art. Dalí declares, "The title *Premonition of Civil War,* which I gave this picture six months before the war broke out, is typical of Dalían prophecy."

In Spain in February the Popular Front of the left wins the election but in July Francisco Franco's military revolt in Morocco marks the beginning of the Civil War. Federico García Lorca killed by Franco's men near Granada.

1937

Dalí's first visit to Italy (he made two others in 1939) confirms his interest in classical art and the Renaissance (especially Raphael) and the baroque.

He writes *The Metamorphosis of Narcissus* (Editions Surréalistes, Paris, and Julian Levy, New York), a "paranoiac poem" illustrating the theme of the double image treated in a painting of the same title.

He paints *The Metamorphosis of Narcissus* (1936–37, Edward F. W. James collection, Tate Gallery, London; *Portrait of Freud,* 1936–37, Gala-Dalí; *Autumnal Cannibalism,* 1936–37, Edward F. W. James collection, Sussex, England; *Sleep,* Edward F. W. James collection, Sussex, England.

He explains *The Metamorphosis of Narcissus:* "A way of visualizing the course of the metamorphoses of Narcissus. If you stare for a while at the hypnotically immobile figure of Narcissus from a short distance and with a certain willed abstraction, it gradually fades away until it is completely invisible. The metamorphosis of the myth is fulfilled at this precise moment because the image of Narcissus is suddenly transformed into the image of a hand that rises out of its reflection. The hand holds an egg

in the fingertips, a seed, the bulb from which the new Narcissus is born—the flowers. About *Autumnal Cannibalism:* "These Iberian creatures devour each other in turn in the autumn and express the pathos of civil war seen as a phenomenon of natural history."

Pablo Picasso paints *Guernica,* the huge painting inspired by the tragic bombing of a small Spanish town and engraves the series of etchings *Sueño y mentira de Franco:* surrealism is used to express the voice of the "other Spain," free Spain.

1938

He participates in the great surrealist exhibition at the Galerie des Beaux-Arts in Paris. He travels to Europe, opens a studio in Rome, and in London meets Sigmund Freud through an introduction by the writer Stefan Zweig.

He illustrates *Cours naturel* by Paul Eluard. He paints *Spagna,* Edward F. W. James collection, Sussex, England; *The Infinite Mystery,* private collection, New York.

In a letter dated July 20, 1938, Sigmund Freud writes: "Up until now I was inclined to consider the surrealists, who had chosen me as their patron, completely mad, or 95 percent like alcohol. . . . The young Spaniard with his deeply sincere and fanatical eyes and undeniable technical skill has made me think again. It would certainly be interesting to make an analysis of the origins of this sort of painting. And yet as a critic one should have the right to say that the concept of art resists being extended beyond the point in which the quantitative relationship between the unconscious material and preconscious work on the subject is not maintained within definite limits."

1939

Dalí works very hard in New York for the surrealist project *The Dream of Venus* for the New York World's Fair, and publishes the *Declaration of Independence of the Imagination and of Man's Right to Madness* to defend the insertion of a fish's head on a Botticelli body as part of the project. The ballet *Bacchanale* is produced at the Metropolitan with scenery and stage design by Dalí: with a dramatic gesture he breaks a plate-glass window at Bonwit Teller to protest against the way in which they carried out his instructions for a window display.

Dalí's work is from now on the opposite of surrealism.

In Spain on March 28, Franco's Nationalist troops enter Madrid and a blood bath ends the Civil War. On September 1, Hitler invades Poland, which leads to the outbreak of the Second World War.

1940

Shortly after the Nazi invasion Dalí leaves Paris and takes refuge in the U.S. via Spain. He remains there until 1948 with a studio at Pebble Beach, California.

He paints *Slave Market with an Apparition of an Invisible Bust of Voltaire*, Salvador Dalí Foundation, Inc., St. Petersburg, Florida; *The Face of War*, Museum Boymans-van Beuningen, Rotterdam.

On June 14 the German troops enter Paris.

1941

He continues his theatrical activities working on the scenery for the ballet *Labyrinth*. At the end of the year his first great retrospective opens at the Museum of Modern Art in New York (forty-three paintings and seventeen drawings).

Breton writes about Dalí in *Artistic Genesis and Perspective of Surrealism:* "In spite of his undeniable talent for self-advertisement, Dalí's undertaking is badly served by his ultraretrograde technique (a return to Meissonier) and discredited by his cynical indifference as to his methods of attracting attention. He has for some time shown signs of panic and only saved himself momentarily, as far as it appears, by his own vulgarization."

1942

In this and the following year Dalí's retrospective is shown in eight American cities; he publishes his biography *The Secret Life of Salvador Dalí* on this wave of success (Dial Press, New York).

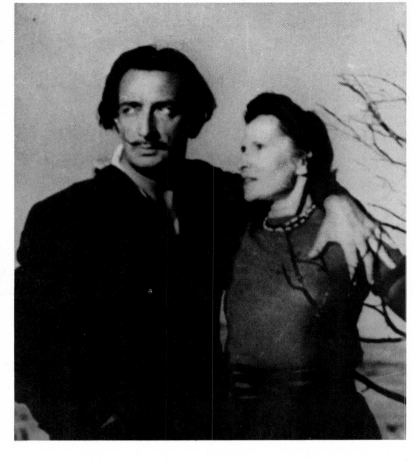

1943

Now one of the myths of American society, Dalí works on a project for interior design, either real (wall panels for Helena Rubenstein's apartment in New York) or imaginary (Mae West's face used as an apartment).

He exhibits twenty-nine works presented by M. Knoedler & Co. of New York.

With his typically protean and open-minded capacity for change he reacts to the crisis in surrealism and the progress of abstract art by claiming, "I intend to become classical." He paints *Geopolitical Child Watching the Birth of New Man*, Salvador Dalí Foundation, Inc., St. Petersburg, Florida.

1944

Dalí spends much time working on the design and production of ballet sequences *El café de chinitas, Sentimental Colloquy,* and *Mad Tristan,* publishes the novel *Hidden Faces* (Dial Press), and illustrates many books, including *Fantastic Memories* by Maurice Sandoz.

He paints *A Minute Before Waking Up from a Dream Provoked by a Bee Flying Around a Pomegranate,* Bruno Pagliari collection, Mexico.

1945

He illustrates *The Maze* by Maurice Sandoz. From now on his work has no connection with the surrealist movement.

Gala and Dalí.

He paints *Apotheosis of Homer*, private collection, Paris; *Three Apparitions of Gala's Face*, Gala-Dalí; *Galarina*, Teatro Museo Dalí, Figueras; *The Bread Basket*, Teatro Museo Dalí, Figueras.

On August 6 the atomic explosion in Hiroshima marks with horror the end of the Second World War.

1946

Dalí illustrates Shakespeare's *Macbeth*. First series of illustrations for Cervantes' *Don Quixote* (Modern Library), followed by another three series, the last in 1965. He paints the scenery for the dream sequences in Alfred Hitchcock's film *Spellbound* and paints *The Temptations of St. Anthony*, Musées Royaux des Beaux-Arts, Brussels.

1947

Dalí illustrates Montaigne's *Essays*.

1948

Dalí returns to Spain and settles at Port Lligat in his house-studio-sanctuary that gradually expands like a living organism over the years with new "cells" added on. He begins studying for his new "classical" phase, and from now on has no connections with postwar avant-garde trends, but finds inspiration in the traditional themes of Western art.

He illustrates *Fifty Secrets of Magic Craftsmanship*, Shakespeare's *As You Like It*, and *The Autobiography of Benvenuto Cellini*.

He said of his house at Port Lligat, "Our house has grown like a real biological structure by gemmation. A new cell is born at every turning point in our life."

1949

First studies for paintings of religious subjects. Dalí's interest in theories of harmony and geometry dates from this year and he studies Luca Pacioli's treatise on divine proportion, but his aim is for a mystic symbolism. He collaborates with a famous mathematician to assure the geometrical perfection of his painting *Léda Atomica*.

He paints *Léda Atomica*, Teatro Museo Dalí, Figueras.

1950

He works on two versions of his first sacred painting, *The Madonna of Port Lligat* (officially approved by the Vatican). Dalí's personal mythology is still obvious in his work.

He paints *Landscape of Port Lligat*, Salvador Dalí Foundation, Inc., St. Petersburg, Florida; *The Madonna of Port Lligat*, Lady J. Dunn Collection, Quebec; *Dalí at the Age of Six When He Thought He Was a Girl, Lifting the Skin of the Water to See a Dog Sleeping in the Shadow of the Sea*, François de Vallombreuse Collection, Paris.

1951

Writes the *Mystic Manifesto* (R. J. Godet, Paris), showing amazing nonchalance at a time of cold war and international tension as he outlines the theory of a nuclear mysticism and "atomic art." He produces the first works of the "nuclear period" in which disintegration of form into particles is shown as spiritual continuity when matter ends.

He paints the *Christ of St. John of the Cross*, Glasgow Art Gallery and Museum; *Exploding Head in the Style of Raphael*, Stead H. Stead-Ellis Collection, Somerset, England; *The Eye of Time*, brooch, 1951–52, Owen Cheatham Foundation, New York; *Mouth*, gold, emerald, and pearl brooch, 1951–52, Owen Cheatham Foundation, New York.

1952

He explains in a series of lectures the significance of his new "mystic nuclear art" and the French translation of his autobiography comes out *("La Vie secrète de Salvador Dalí*, La Table Ronde, Paris).

He prepares 102 watercolours to illustrate Dante's *Divine Comedy*.

He paints *Galatea with Spheres*, private collection, New York; *Assumptacorpuscularialapislazulina*, John Theodoracopulos Collection; *Nuclear Cross*, Galerie F. Petit, Paris.

1954

Dalí's first important retrospective in Rome, Italy (24 paintings, 17 drawings, and 102 watercolours illustrating the *Divine Comedy*).

He publishes *Dalí's Moustache* with Philippe Halsmann (Simon & Schuster, New York).

He studies *Discourses on the Cube* by Juan de Herrera, the great architect of the Escorial, and follows his precepts in his painting *Corpus Hypercubicus*. He identifies the obsession with rhinoceros horn with the same reflections (the disintegrated particles assume the shape of a rhinoceros horn), as it is unique among living things in having a perfect logarithmical spiral.

He paints *Rhinocerontic Disintegration of Phidias Ilissos*, private collection, New York; *Corpus Hypercubicus*, Chester Dale collection, Metropolitan Museum of Art, New York.

1955

Returns to a study of old masters, particularly Vermeer, and completes a large religious painting, *The Last Supper*, designed according to the dodecahedral structure and with symbolic reference to the number twelve.

He paints *Paranoiac-critical Study of Vermeer's Lacemaker*, private collection; *The Supper*, Chester Dale collection, National Gallery of Art, Washington.

1956

Big retrospective exhibition at Knokke-le-Zoute in Belgium (34 oils, 48 drawings and watercolours): the first not to be set up by Dalí himself.

He writes an unusual and provocative treatise on modern art, *Les Cocus du vieil art moderne* (Fasquelle, Paris, English edition entitled *Dalí on Modern Art,* Dial Press, New York, 1957).

He paints *Rhinocerontic Gooseflesh,* Bruno Pagliari collection, Mexico; *Nature Morte Vivante (Still Life Fast Moving),* Salvador Dalí Foundation, Inc., St. Petersburg, Florida; *The Skull of Zurbarán,* J. H. Hirshhorn Foundation, New York.

He declares, "The ultraretrograde technique of Meissonier is best suited to represent ultramodern biological and nuclear subjects."

1957–59

He continues to explore old masters (Velázquez), and religious themes which lead him to study the great historical themes of Western art. At the same time with his natural ability for being involved in artistic or commercial projects that catch on in a big way, Dalí shows an interest in "optical art" and uses it to achieve unusual optical illusions.

He paints *Santiago the Great,* 1957, Lord Beaverbrook collection, Fredericton Gallery of Art, Canada; *Velázquez Painting the Infanta Margarita with the Light and Shadow of His Own Glory,* 1958, Salvador Dalí Foundation, Inc., St. Petersburg, Florida; *Ear with Madonna,* 1958, Mr. and Mrs. H. J. Heinz Collection, Museum of Modern Art, New York; *The Virgin of Guadalupe,* 1959, Alfonso Fierro Collection, Madrid; *The Discovery of America by Christopher Columbus,* 1959, Salvador Dalí Foundation, Inc., St. Petersburg, Florida.

He wrote about the *Santiago the Great,* "Painting for the first time an antiexistentialist tremor, the tremor of national unity. Everything in this painting comes from the four jasmine petals that explode into a creative atomic cloud"; and of the *Ear with Madonna,* "Two meters away it looks like Raphael's Sistine Madonna, at fifteen meters it is the ear of an angel one and a half meters high, painted with antimatter and thus pure energy."

1960

He illustrates with various techniques *The Apocalypse of St. John,* including a miniature on copper with touches of gold, published in a single edition in 1961 by Joseph Foret, Paris.

He begins working with Robert Descharnes on the book *The World of Salvador Dalí,* published in 1962 (Edita S.A., Lausanne).

Dalí's interest in historical subjects leads him back yet again to a striking revival of nineteenth-century historical painting, especially in the style of his fellow countryman Mariano Fortuny, and he makes many sketches and gouaches of his monumental *Battle of Tetuán* from 1960 to 1961 in the Museum of Barcelona.

He completes his largest religious canvas, *The Ecumenical Council,* private collection. He paints Gala again, *Gala Nude Seen from Behind,* Teatro Museo Dalí, Figueras; *Hyperxylogical Sky,* Gala-Dalí.

1961

Two ballets produced in Venice (including *Ballet de Gala*) with scenes and costumes by Dalí.

A new enlarged edition of his autobiography published (Dial Press, New York, and Vision Press, London). The Egg Room, entirely created and furnished by Gala and dedicated to the myth of Leda, is the last "cell" added to the house at Port Lligat.

1962

From now on Dalí's work concentrates increasingly on returning to the themes and techniques of his past, reconsidered according to modern developments such as American pop art experiments, and also inspired by sensational technical and scientific discoveries.

He paints *The Battle of Tetuán,* 1961–62, David Nahonad Collection, Milan; *The Christ of El Vallès,* Giuseppe Albaretto Collection, Turin.

F. H. C. Crick, J. D. Watson, and M. H. F. Wilkins receive the Nobel Prize for Physiology and Medicine for their studies on DNA (deoxyribonucleic acid), the "molecule of life."

1963

He publishes *Le Mythe Tragique de l'Angélus de Millet* (J. J. Pauvert, Paris), a "paranoiac-critical" interpretation of Millet's masterpiece.

As in the background of *The Battle of Tetuán,* Dalí's paintings of this period show Crick and Watson's double helix model of the molecular structure.

He paints *Portrait of My Dead Brother,* private collection, New York; *Galacideoxyribonucleic,* New England Merchants National Bank, Boston.

1964

Big Dalí retrospective at Tokyo organized by the *Mainichi Newspaper.*

He publishes *Le Journal d'un génie* (La Table Ronde, Paris; abridged American edition, Doubleday, New York, 1965). He begins the fourth series of illustrations for *Don Quixote* for the Italian magazine *Tempo* and finishes them in 1965.

Photomontage, 1948, in which Philippe Halsmann has tried to interpret Dalí's world (above). Below, the painter leans confidentially and questioningly towards a wooden statue of a saint.

1965

Important retrospective at the Gallery of Modern Art in New York (170 paintings, 59 drawings, gouaches, and watercolours, 10 engravings, 18 objects and sculptures), including the A. Reynolds Morse collection, exhibited for the first time in public.

He begins working on "three-dimensional" themes which he carries on over the next few years.

He paints 100 watercolours to illustrate the Bible, and a series of pen drawings for *The Erotic Metamorphoses* (Editions à l'Erotidiade, Lausanne).

He paints *Salvador Dalí in the Act of Painting Gala in the Apotheosis of the Dollar*, private collection, New York; *Gala Contemplating Dalí in a State of Levitation Above His "Pop, Op, Yes, Yes, Pompier*," private collection, New York; *Bust of Dante*, bronze, numbered edition of six.

He declares: "In modern esthetics one can say that POP ART (of which the supreme ideal is hand-made photographs) plus OP ART (its supreme ideal is cybernetic "moiré"), produces the supreme ART POMPIER, as used by Meissonier. . . ."

1966–67

The film *Autoportrait mou de Salvador Dalí* (1966) is made at Port Lligat.

He paints *Tuna Fishing* (1966–67), Paul Ricard Foundation, Paris.

For the Expo '67 at Montreal Buckminster Fuller designs the great geodesic dome called the biosphere, which was inspired by molecular structures.

1968

Dalí begins collecting notes for his book *The Art of History*. He is in Paris during the events of May and writes *My Cultural Revolution*. ""L'art est mort, ne consommez pas son cadavre!" (graffito on the walls of the Sorbonne during the May occupation).

1969

His theories of the new "art pompier" lead Dalí away from the big pictures of the preceding period to real monumental art. The first work is a ceiling three meters in diameter in the Alleuis palace in Barcelona, painted with *The Royal Hour*.

He paints *Portrait of Gala*, in the Teatro Museo Dalí, Figueras.

1970

He designs another ceiling for the castle of Pubol, which he has given to Gala. Continuing his research on "three-dimensional art," he studies the Dutch artist Gerard Dou,

Vermeer's contemporary, and discovers that some of his paintings are "stereoscopic" (i.e., they have a double image); he tries to create stereoscopic images using a Fresnel lens and his interest in holography dates from this time. He presents the French president Georges Pompidou with *The Funerary Mask of Napoleon,* a "tomb-plinth that contains the maximum of imperialist strength."

He engraves a series of eleven plates for the *Hippies* series.

First plans and early work on the Teatro Museo Dalí at Figueras in collaboration with the Spanish architect Emilio Pérez Piñero.

He paints *Hallucinogenic Toreador,* 1969–70, Salvador Dalí Foundation, Inc., St. Petersburg, Florida; *The Funerary Mask of Napoleon,* gilded bronze, 1970, private collection, Paris.

1971

Dalí's research into spatial values and the pictorial expression of the third dimension concentrates on the study of holography (a hologram is an optical-reticular image of an object illuminated by a laser beam that gives the total illusion of relief).

He engraves a series of plates for *Ten Recipes for Immortality* with two "stereoscopic" plates (Andouin-Descharnes, Paris) and designs and starts work on the ceiling of the foyer of the Teatro Museo Dalí at Figueras.

The American physicist Dennis Gabor is awarded the Nobel Prize for discovering the use of laser beams and holography.

1972

On the advice of Dennis Gabor, Dalí makes three holographic compositions *(Polyhydras, Underwater Fisherman, Olà, Olà, Velázquez! Gabor!),* exhibited at the Knoedler Gallery in New York.

He declares, "Three-dimensional reality has interested all artists from Velázquez onwards and Picasso's analytical cubism in modern times has attempted to capture Velázquez's three dimensions. Now thanks to Gabor's genius an artistic renaissance is possible and the doors are open to a new creative field for me to work in."

1974

In September the Teatro Museo Dalí in Figueras is officially opened. Dalí works on small sculptures and objects in precious materials—gold and silver (exhibited at the Figueras museum). He paints *Ruggero Liberating Angelica, Transformation, Anchorite, Figure from Behind, Explosion of Faith in a Cathedral, Angels Watching the Ordination of a Saint* (all in the Teatro Museo Dalí, Figueras).

1975–76

He goes back to making stereoscopic pictures and creates *Stereoscopic Painting,* 1976, Teatro Museo Dalí, Figueras.

He declares, "I have always been an anarchist and monarchist at the same time. A true cultural revolution is the restoration of monarchist principles. The monarchist tradition is change and reinvention and is translated in painting into the use of an ultraphotographic technique."

On November 20, 1975, Francisco Franco dies after nearly forty years of dictatorship, having previously arranged for the restoration of the monarchy, designating Prince Juan Carlos as his successor.

Photomontage of Dalí at the feet of Christ in his Christ of St. John of the Cross, *painted in 1951.*

Art for Looking at One's Soul

*68 works
by Salvador Dalí*

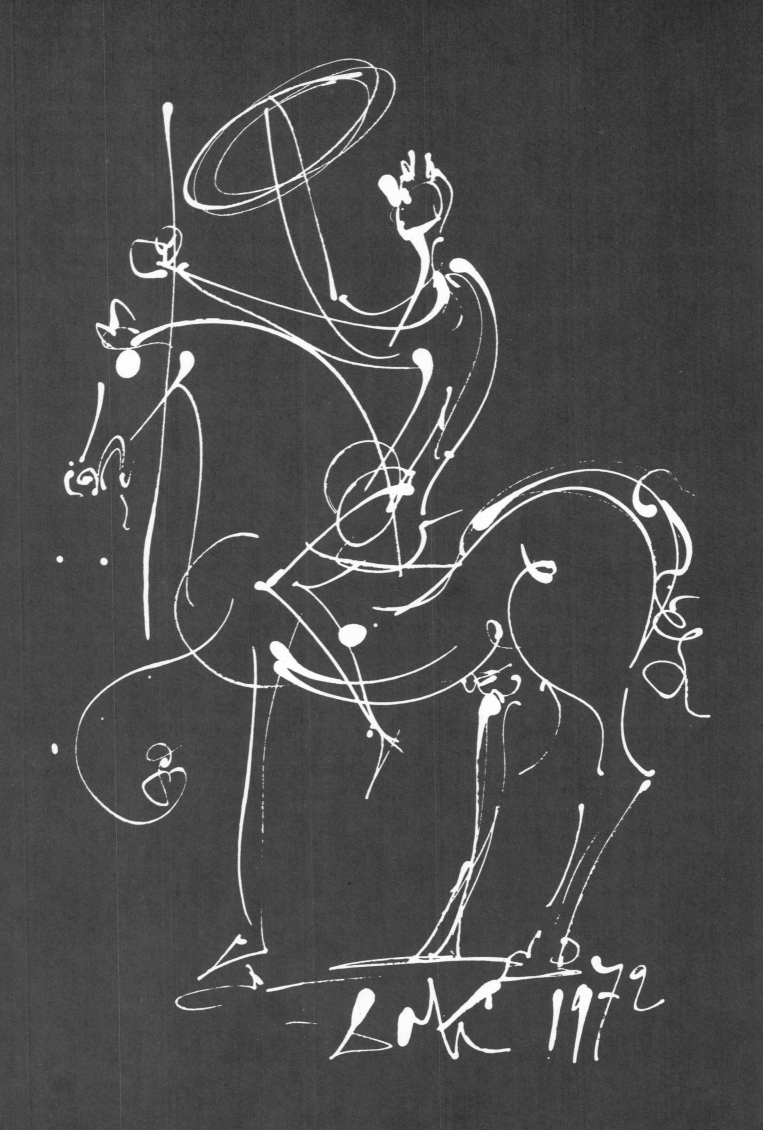

Self-portrait with Neck of Raphael (1922–23), oil on canvas (54 × 57 cm / 21 × 22⅜ in), private collection, Paris. On the following pages: *Cadaqués* (1922), oil on canvas (60.5 × 82 cm / 23 6/8 × 32⅜ in), Montserrat Dalí collection, Barcelona. *Aunt Ana Sewing in Cadaqués* (1916–1917), oil on sackcloth (48 × 62 cm / 18⅞ × 24⅜ in) Joaquín Vila-Moners collection, Figueras. *Self-portrait Splitting into Three* (1927), oil on cardboard (70 × 50 cm / 27½ × 19¾ in) Teatro Museo Dalí, Figueras. Dalí's favourite artists, in addition to Raphael, are Leonardo, Bosch, Velázquez, Goya, Vermeer, Meissonier, and Millet. "Raphael is the painter. In my autobiography, between chapters entitled 'Against Spinach and for Snails' and 'Against Buddha and for the Marquis de Sade,' there is one entitled 'Against Michelangelo and for Raphael,' " Dalí declared in an interview published in Rome in the 1950s. His autobiography was published in England as *The Secret Life of Salvador Dalí.*

Muchachas (circa 1923), tempera on cardboard (105 × 75 cm / 41⅜ × 29½ in). Teatro Museo Dalí, Figueras. Following pages: *The First Days of Spring* (1922–1923), India ink and watercolour on paper (21.5 × 15.5 cm / 8½ × 6⅛ in), Ramón Estalella collection, Madrid; *Figure of a Woman* (circa 1926), oil on canvas (61 × 38 cm / 24 × 15 in), Teatro Museo Dalí, Figueras. Before turning to surrealism around 1927, Dalí was influenced by different schools and assimilated impressionism and the Fauves, the metaphysical painting of de Chirico and Carrà, and had even been interested in futurism and cubism. The negation of perspective learned from Leonardo was finally the basis of Dalí's geometric concept of painting.

Purist Still Life (1924), oil on canvas (100 × 100 cm / 39⅜ × 39⅜ in), Teatro Museo Dalí, Figueras. Following pages: *Girl Seen from Behind* (1925), oil on canvas (108 × 77 cm / 42½ × 30⅜ in) Museo Español de Arte Contemporáneo, Madrid. *Girl Seen from Behind Looking Out of the Window* (1925), oil on canvas (103 × 74 cm / 40½ × 29⅛ in), Museo Español de Arte Contemporáneo, Madrid. Cadaqués and Port Lligat, places, are, like Gala, a person, reference points in Dalí's work, even when the houses are shown as syphons and dishes or the church of Cadaqués is a cubist guitar. Dalí considered Port Lligat "one of the most arid places . . . on the earth. The mornings are of a savage and bitter, ferociously analytical and structural gaiety; the evenings often become morbidly melancholy."

Port Alguer (1925), oil on canvas (36 × 38 cm / 14¼ × 15 in), private collection. Following pages: *Putrefied Birds* (circa 1928), oil and collage on panel (50 × 65 cm / 19 6/8 × 25⅜ in), Teatro Museo Dalí, Figueras. *Torso* (circa 1928), oil on panel (76 × 63 cm / 29⅞ × 24⅞ in), Teatro Museo Dalí, Figueras. *Head of a Woman* (1927), oil on canvas (100 × 100 cm / 39⅜ × 39⅜ in), Teatro Museo Dalí, Figueras. *Inaugural Gooseflesh* (1928), oil on canvas (75.5 × 62.5 cm / 29¾ × 24½ in), Ramón Pichot collection, Barcelona. Dalí loved to watch the fishermen, "the mad fishermen of this village," from the inaccessible cliffs of Cabo Creus and await their return to Port Alguer or Port Lligat in the sunset, and then listen to their arguments in their rich argot and then return home with Gala, who had sometimes been out fishing herself.

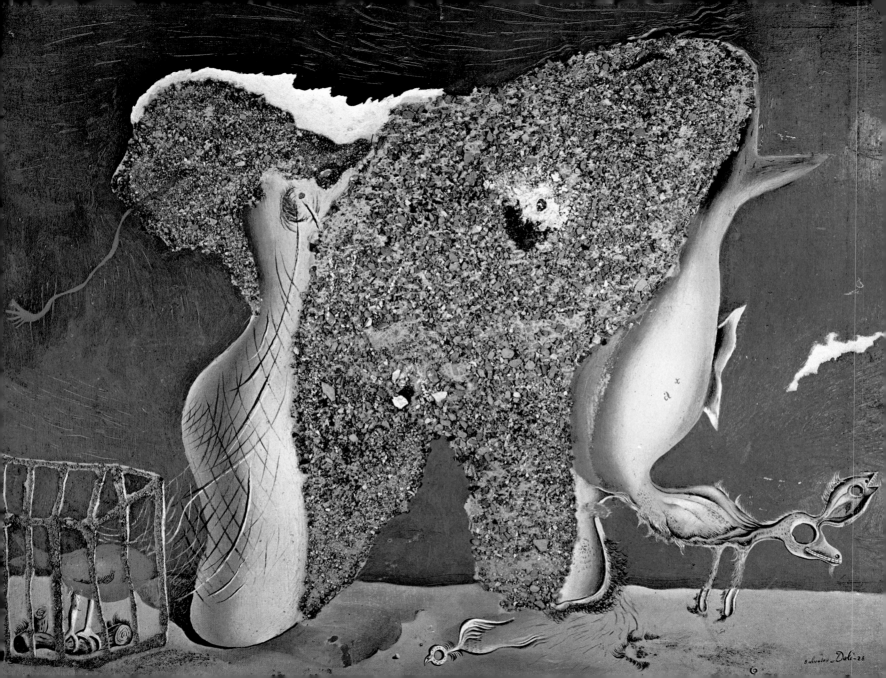

Perspective (1936), oil on canvas (65 × 65.5 cm / 25⅜ × 25¾ in), E. Hoffmann Foundation, Kunstmuseum, Basel. Following pages: *Portrait of Gala* (1931), oil on paper (14 × 9 cm / 5½ × 3⅝ in), Albert Field collection, New York; *Ghosts of Two Automobiles* (circa 1929), collage and oil on card, Teatro Museo Dalí, Figueras. "Profession: genius" is how the press paraphrased Dalí's opinion of himself. He claimed that his genius lay in his "paranoiac-critical method," "a spontaneous method of irrational knowledge based on the interpretive-critical association of delirious phenomena" which helps to control madness through painting (hallucinations, obsessions, visions), by its mastery of the dividing line between reality and imagination." "The difference between me and a madman is that I am not mad."

The Specter of Sex Appeal (1934), oil on canvas (17 × 13 cm / 6⅝ × 5⅛ in), Teatro Museo Dalí, Figueras. Following pages: *Three Young Surrealist Women Holding in their Arms the Skins of an Orchestra* (1936), oil on canvas (54 × 65 cm / 21¼ × 25⅜ in); Salvador Dalí Foundation, Inc., St. Petersburg, Florida. From childhood Dalí suffered from obsessions and fears and his "paranoiac-critical method" is Freudian in origin. Perhaps his concept of hyperreality lies also in his desire to show human nature in all its contradictions, and he cultivated a special image and behaviour (it could be called exhibitionism) dictated by a constant obsession with the theme of death.

Soft Construction with Cooked Beans—Premonition of Civil War (1936), oil on canvas (100 × 99 cm / 39⅜ × 39 in), Louise and Walter Arensberg collection, Philadelphia Museum of Art. Following pages: *The Chemist of Figueras Looking for Nothing at All* (1936), oil on wood panel (30 × 56 cm / 11⅞ × 22 in), Edward F. W. James collection, Sussex, England. Dalí claimed he received intuitions and revelations on even the most common subjects and declared these to all the world: "The title *Premonition of Civil War,* which I gave this picture six months before war broke out, is a typical example of Dalían prophecy." And a critic wrote, "At a time when one cannot rely on the reality and authenticity of pseudo revelations that all come to much the same in the end, Dalí's genius is great enough to transcend space and time."

Above: *Geological Justice* (1936), oil on wood panel (11 × 19 cm / 4⅜ × 7½ in), Edward F. W. James collection, Sussex, England; below: detail of *Solar Table* (1936), Edward F. W. James Foundation, Brighton Art Gallery. Following pages: *Spain* (1938), oil on canvas (92 × 60 cm / 36¼ × 23⅝ in), Edward F. W. James collection, Sussex, England; *Rhinocerontic Gooseflesh* (1956), oil on canvas (93 × 60 cm / 36⅝ × 23⅝ in), Bruno Paliari collection, Mexico. *The Infinite Mystery* (1938), oil on textile (114 × 146 cm / 45 × 57½ in), private collection, New York. "All his life Dalí was fascinated by objects that resembled something they are not" (R. Descharnes). The rhinoceros horn is a perfect spiral and Dalí "reflected on this problem" a lot.

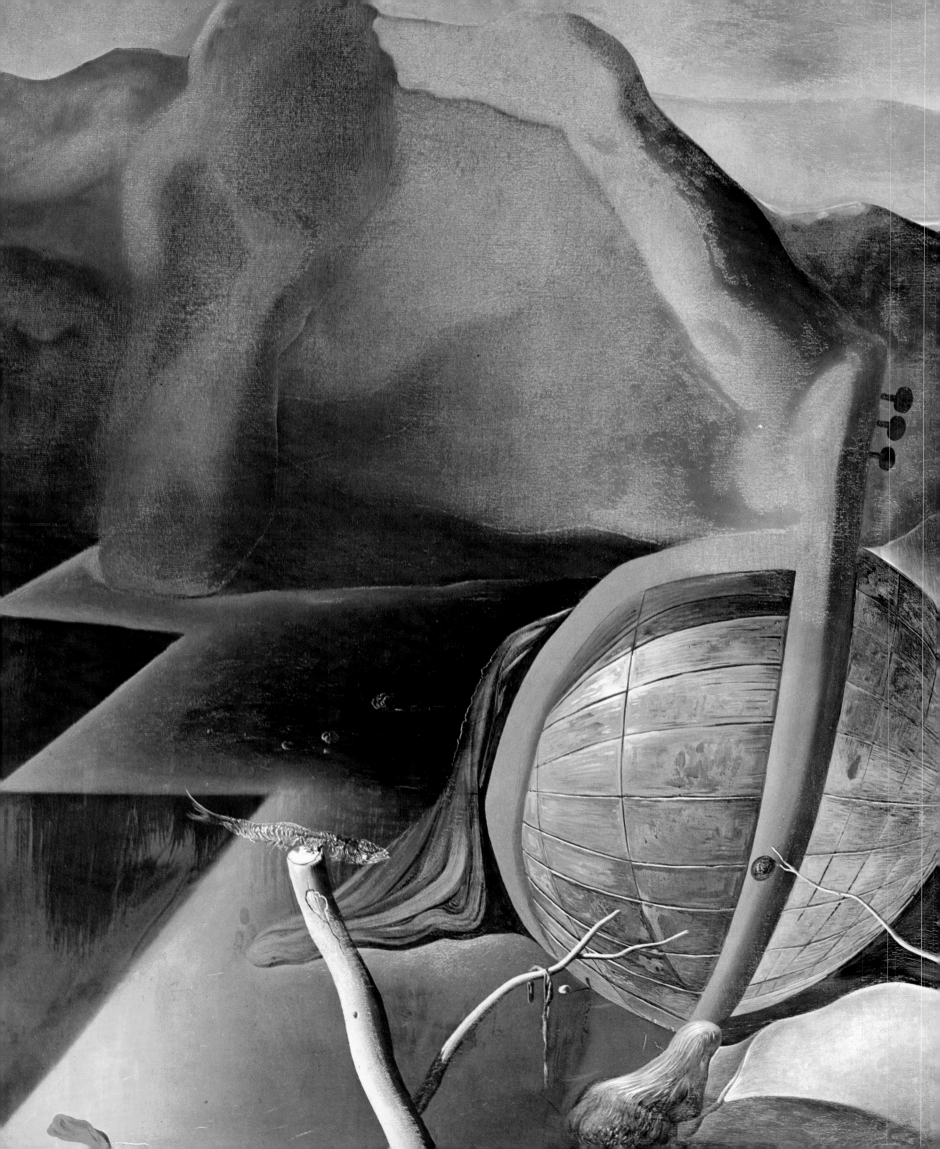

Detail from *Sleep* (1937), oil on canvas (51 × 78 cm / 20⅛ × 30¾ in), Edward F. W. James Collection, Sussex, England. Following pages: Detail of *Autumnal Cannibalism* (1936–37), oil on canvas (80 × 80 cm / 31½ × 31½ in), Edward F. W. James Collection, Sussex, England. *Galarina* (1945), oil on canvas (65 × 50 cm / 25⅜ × 19¾ in), Teatro Museo Dalí, Figueras. "Since sleep is possible, we need a whole system of crutches in psychic equilibrium. Only one would not be enough as we would wake up and the little boat in particular would at once disappear." "These Iberian creatures taking turns devouring each other in autumn express the pathos of civil war considered as a phenomenon of natural history"—these are the comments "pronounced in writing" of Dalí on this painting and those on the following pages. Gala is wife, companion, sister, mother, nurse, model, inspiration, and Madonna at the same time.

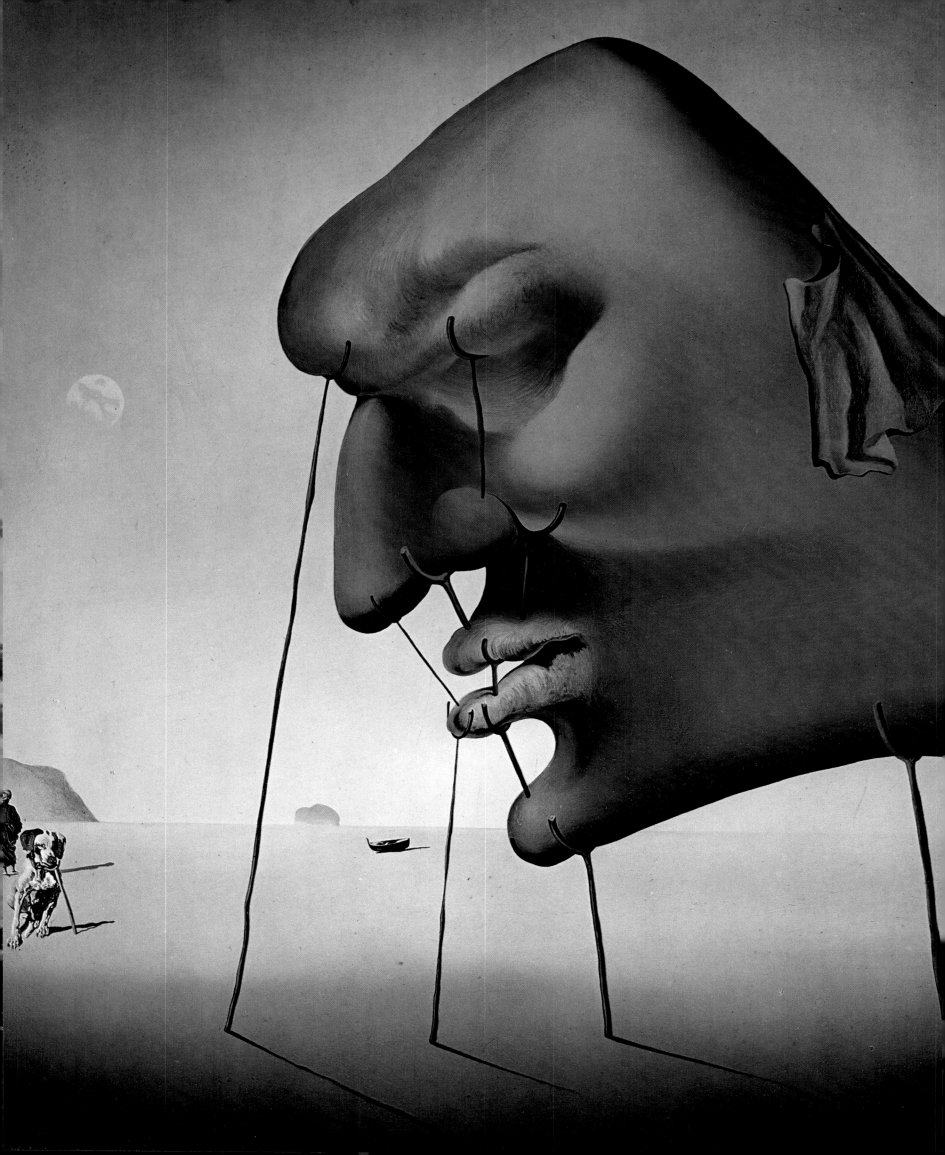

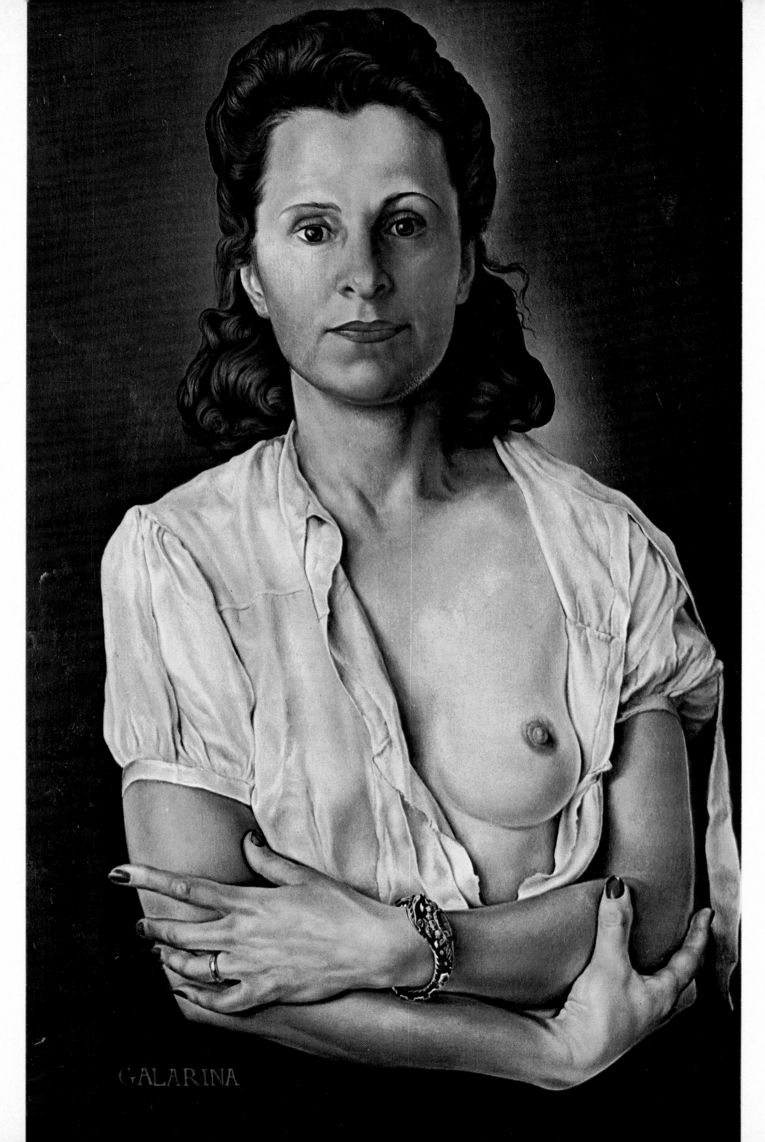

GALARINA

Atomic Leda (1949), oil on canvas (60 × 44 cm / 23⅝ × 17⅜ in), Teatro Museo Dalí, Figueras. Following pages: *Dalí at the Age of Six When He Thought He Was a Girl, Lifting the Skin of the Water to See a Dog Sleeping in the Shadow of the Sea* (1950), oil on canvas (27 × 34 cm / 10⅝ × 13⅜ in), François Vallombreuse collection, Paris. Gala is the mother and mystical symbol, also the "surrealist muse." For others besides Dalí she personified the myth of Leda, the mortal mother of the brothers Castor and Pollux, the former mortal and the latter immortal because he was fathered by Zeus in the form of a swan. Dalí brings this myth up to date, showing his own life and that of his dead brother, both to identify with the story and to liberate himself from it.

Galatea of the Spheres (1952), oil on canvas (65 × 54 cm / 25⅜ × 21¼ in), private collection, New York. In the following pages: *The Christ of St. John of the Cross* (1951), oil on canvas (205 × 116cm / 80¾ × 45¾ in), Glasgow Art Gallery and Museum. With the "conquest of the irrational" Dalí contrasts his parallel of refusing to work as a subjection of the intelligence to commercial interests, or what the industrial world sees as "reality"—a common theme of the surrealist esthetic; the surrealists' mentor, André Breton, immediately drew attention to Dalí's own greed and pleasure in money from the exploitation of his work, and made up an anagram of Dalí's name, Avida Dollars.

The Madonna of Port Lligat (1950), oil on canvas (366 × 244 cm / 144¼ × 96⅛ in), Lady J. Dunn collection, Quebec. This is one of Dalí's finest works, showing a rare balance of elements. It was painted at the beginning of the atomic age, heralded by the terrifying explosion at Hiroshima, and Dalí was in his atomic period, where all is "suspended, disintegrated, separated," "as if the atomic bomb had exploded" over the whole world, but a mysticism prevails as a thin ray of hope (because of this picture Dalí was presented to the Pope during Holy Year because of his "conversion"), love (Dalí's Madonnas always have the features of his only model, Gala), and transparent optimism, the uncontaminated source of our true origins.

The Bread Basket (1945), oil on canvas (37 × 32 cm / 14⅝ × 12⅝ in),
Teatro Museo Dalí, Figueras. Following pages: detail from *Vertigo*
(1930), oil on canvas (60 × 50 cm / 23⅝ × 19¾ in), Carlo Ponti
collection, Rome; the watch-brooch *The Eye of Time* (1952–52), Owen
Cheatham Foundation, New York; *Mouth,* gold, ruby, and pearl brooch
(1951–52), Owen Cheatham Foundation, New York. *Nature Morte
Vivante (Still Life Fast Moving)* (1956), oil on canvas (125 × 160 cm / 149
× 63 in), Salvador Dalí Foundation, Inc., St. Petersburg, Florida;
Rhinocerontic Disintegration of Phidias Ilissos (1954), oil on canvas (99 ×
126 cm / 39 × 50⅞ in), private collection, New York. "Twenty years after
the basket has become a crown and the bread has achieved the unity of
the elbow or of the rhinoceros's horn" (Dalí).

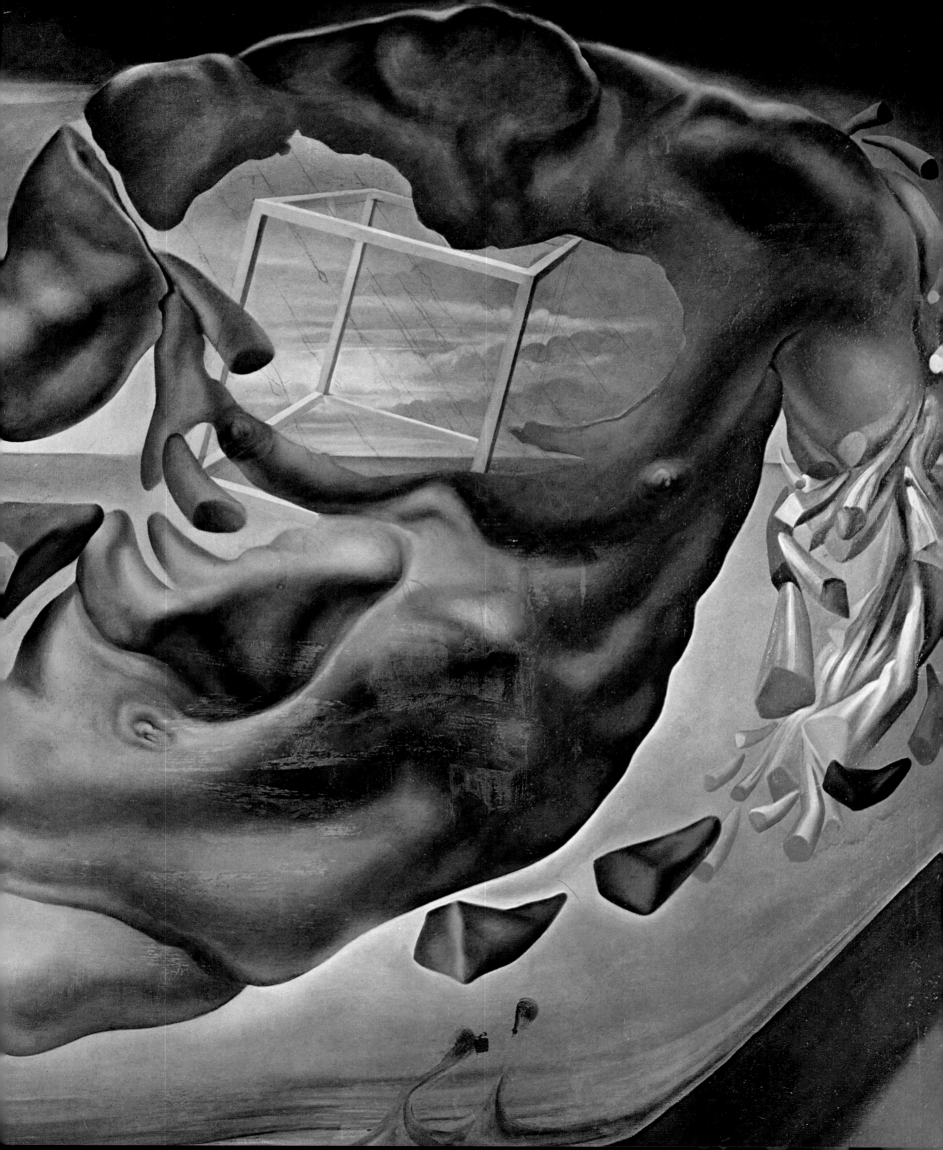

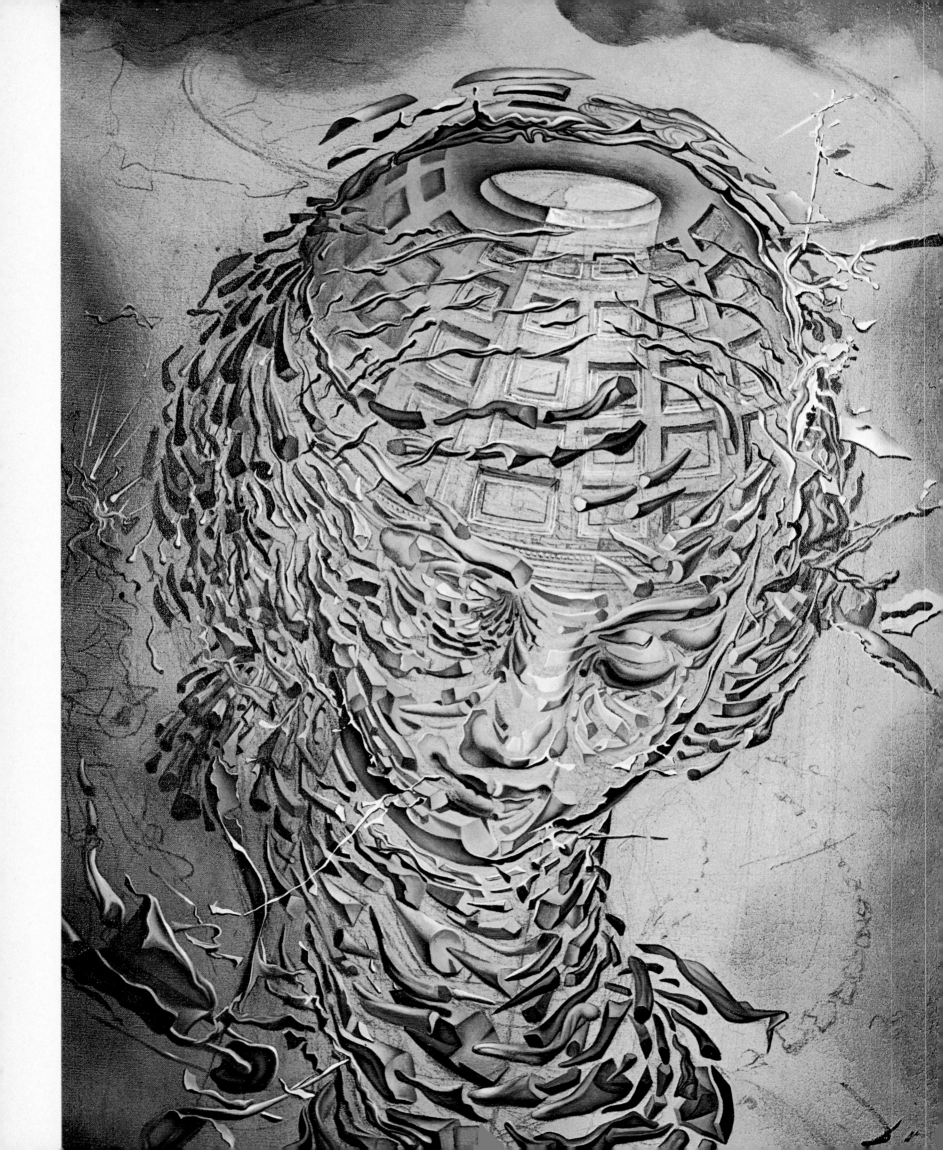

Exploding Head in the Style of Raphael (1951), oil on canvas (67 × 57 cm / 26⅜ × 22⅜ in), Stead H. Stead-Ellis collection, Somerset, England. Following pages: *The Last Supper* (1955), oil on canvas (167 × 268 cm / 65¾ × 105½ in), Chester Dale collection, National Gallery of Art, Washington. Details of *The Last Supper*. "No philosophical, moral, esthetic, or biological revelation enables us to deny God. Even better, the temple whose walls are built by special techniques will not stand without the perfect vault of heaven as its roof." "My mysticism is not only religious, but also nuclear, hallucinatory, the mysticism of Gothic cubism, the mysticism of gold, the mysticism of the railway station of Perpignan and the mysticism of soft watches."

Gala Looking at Christ (1954), oil on canvas (31 × 27 cm / 12⅛ × 10⅝ in), Teatro Museo Dalí, Figueras. Following pages: *Corpus Hypercubicus* (1954), oil on canvas (194 × 124 cm / 76½ × 48⅞ in), Chester Dale collection, Metropolitan Museum of Art, New York. Gala in a detail from *Corpus Hypercubicus. Santiago the Great* (1957), oil on canvas (400 × 300 cm / 157½ × 118¼ in), Lord Beaverbrook collection, Fredericton Gallery of Art, Canada. For almost a decade Dalí had abandoned surrealist ideas for the "rhinoceros horn," for "nuclear mysticism" (his "nuclear period"), and for the "cubic form," but "before surrealism it was possible to observe the intensity of light only through small, unnoticed rays that penetrated like the phrases 'half awake' and 'awakening.' The decisive act of surrealism was to show how they would continue to develop" (André Breton).

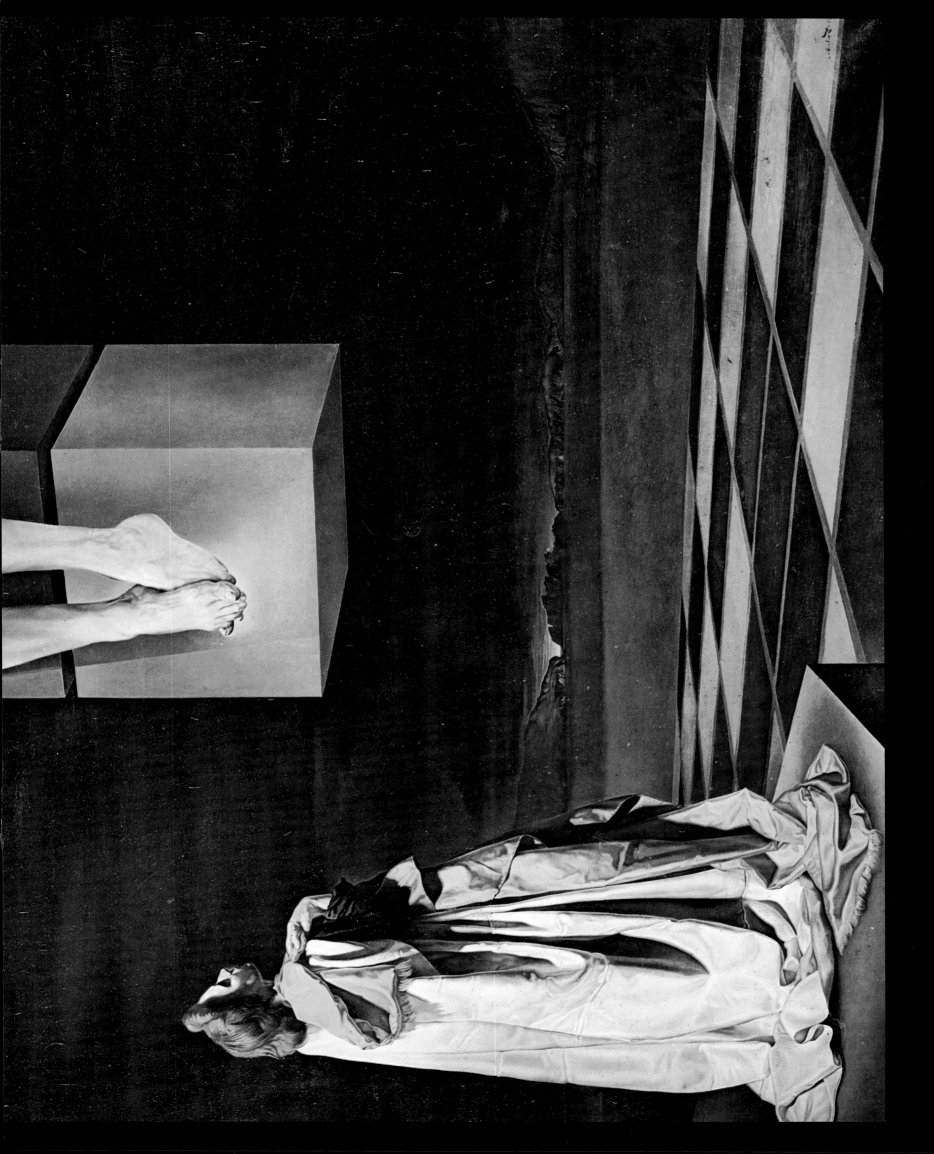

Detail of *Santiago the Great*. Following pages: *Gala Nude Seen from Behind* (1960), oil on canvas (42 × 32 cm / 16½ × 12⅝ in), Teatro Museo Dalí, Figueras. *Velazquez Painting the Infanta Margarita with the Lights and Shadows of his own Glory* (1958), oil on canvas (153 × 92 cm / 60¼ × 36¼ in), Salvador Dalí Foundation, Inc., St. Petersburg, Florida. This is one of many examples of Gala, the recurrent subject of Dalí's work (and he so often signed his paintings Dalí-gala or Gala-Dalí, or a contraction of the two: Galí).

142

143

Stereoscopic Painting (1976), oil on canvas, Teatro Museo Dalí, Figueras. Following pages: Detail and whole of *Discovery of America by Christopher Columbus* (1959), oil on canvas (410 × 310 cm / 161½ × 122 in), Salvador Dalí Foundation, Inc., St. Petersburg, Florida; Gala is again the subject. This was how she was celebrated in a poem by Eluard, who lost his wife to Dalí: "Come, Rise up. Soon the lightest feathers, space suits of the air, will hold you up by the neck. The earth only gives what is necessary and your birds of infinite variety smile. In place of your sadness, like a shadow behind love, the countryside stretches everywhere. Quickly come, run. And your body moves faster than your thoughts and nothing, you understand, nothing can excel you."

Detail of *The Discovery of America by Christopher Columbus.*
Following pages: Another detail of the same picture. *The Virgin of Guadalupe* (1959), oil on canvas (130 × 98.5cm / 51¼ × 38¾ in.), Alfonso Fierro Collection, Madrid. The discovery of America as a paranoic dream presaged, according to Dalí, by Lullo Raimondo, a Catalán metaphysical alchemist whose ideas influenced Dalí's work, and Dr. Ulloa di Figueras, who was tremendously proud of Columbus's Catalán birth. The rocks of Cabo Creus appear with cuneiform geological signs above the standard of the Immaculate Conception (the model is of course Gala), which was planted in the soil of the new land (symbolically shown as an enormous sea urchin with a planet's aureole around it), by Christopher Columbus, a Catalán Jew, being welcomed by St. Narcissus, "patron saint of Gerona and of flies."

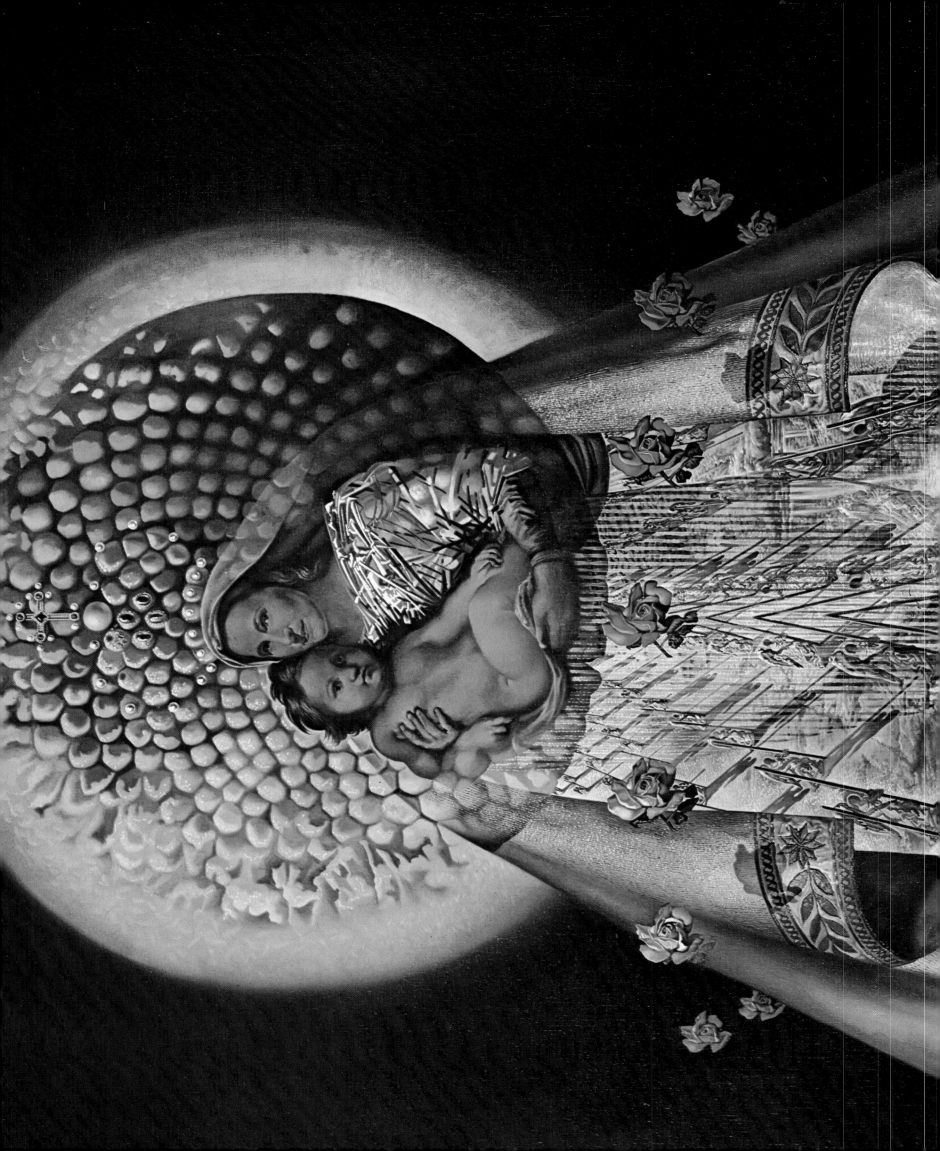

Detail of *The Virgin of Guadalupe*. Following pages: *Battle of Tetuán* (1962), oil on canvas (308 × 406 cm / 121⅜ × 160 in), David Nahonad Collection, Milan. Another detail from the same work. The following quotes are a short summary of the main points of surrealism and Dalí's ideas: "In Breton's vision surrealism can be schematically reduced to the double motive of the experience of contradictions and the practice of a dialectic that aims at overcoming these contradictions" (Ivos Margoni). "The human mind seems to be made so it cannot be incoherent to itself" (Paul Valéry, quoted by Breton in *Les Pas perdus*). But: "Movements begin when a group is formed and end with the dissemination of the personality." (Marcel Duchamp).

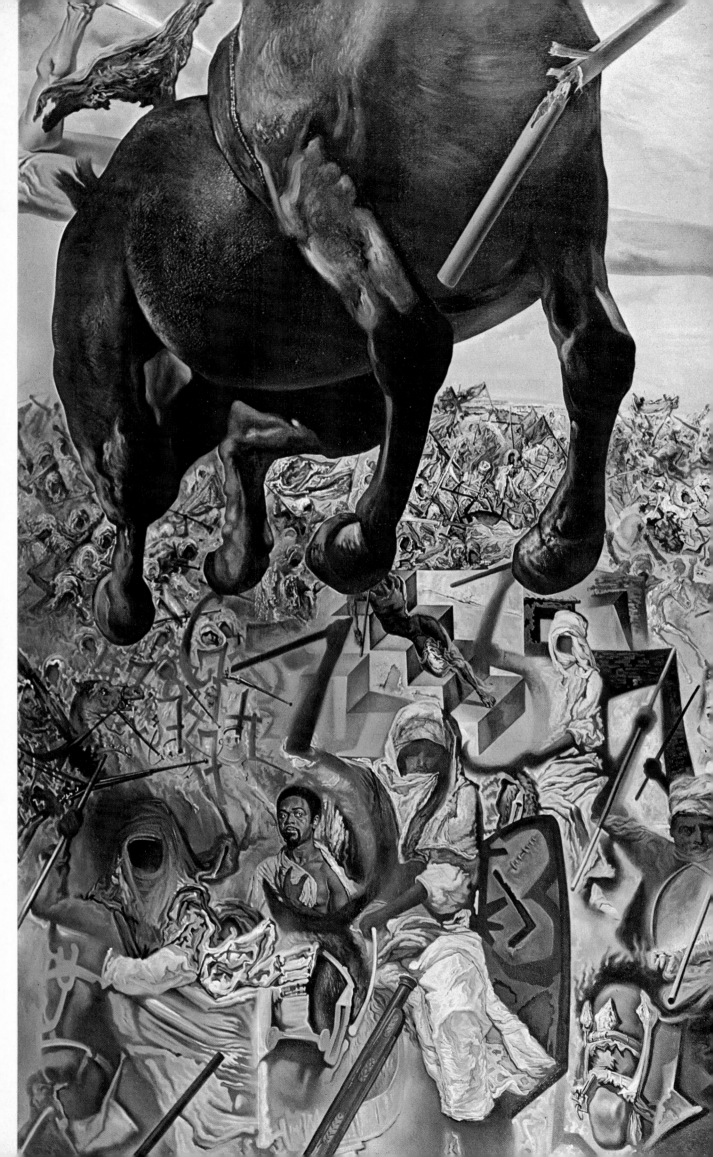

Salvador Dali in the Act of Painting Gala in the Apotheosis of the Dollar, in Which Can Also Be Seen, on the Left, Marcel Duchamp Masked by Louis XIV Behind a Canopy in the Style of Vermeer, Which Is None Other Than the Invisible but Monumental Face of the Hermes of Praxiteles (1965), oil on canvas (400 × 498 cm / 157½ × 196 in), private collection, New York. Following pages: a detail of the same picture. *The Christ of El Vallés* (1962), oil on canvas (92 × 75 cm / 36¼ × 29½ in), Giuseppe Albaretto collection, Turin.

Portrait of My Dead Brother (1963), oil on canvas (175 × 175 cm / 69 × 69 in), private collection, New York. Following pages: *Gala Contemplating Dalí in a State of Levitation Above His "Pop, Op, Yes, Yes, Pompier" Work of Art in Which We Can See the Two Anxious Characters from Millet's Angelus in Atavistic Hibernation in Front of a Sky Which Can Suddenly Transform Itself into a Gigantic Maltese Cross in the Very Center of Perpignan Station, on Which the Whole Universe Is Converging* (1965). Oil on canvas (295 × 406 cm / 116¼ × 160 in), private collection, New York; *Ink Drawing* (1970), Teatro Museo Dalí, Figueras; *Hallucinogenic Toreador* (1969–70), oil on canvas (400 × 300 cm / 157½ × 118¼ in), Salvador Dalí Foundation, Inc., St. Petersburg, Florida.

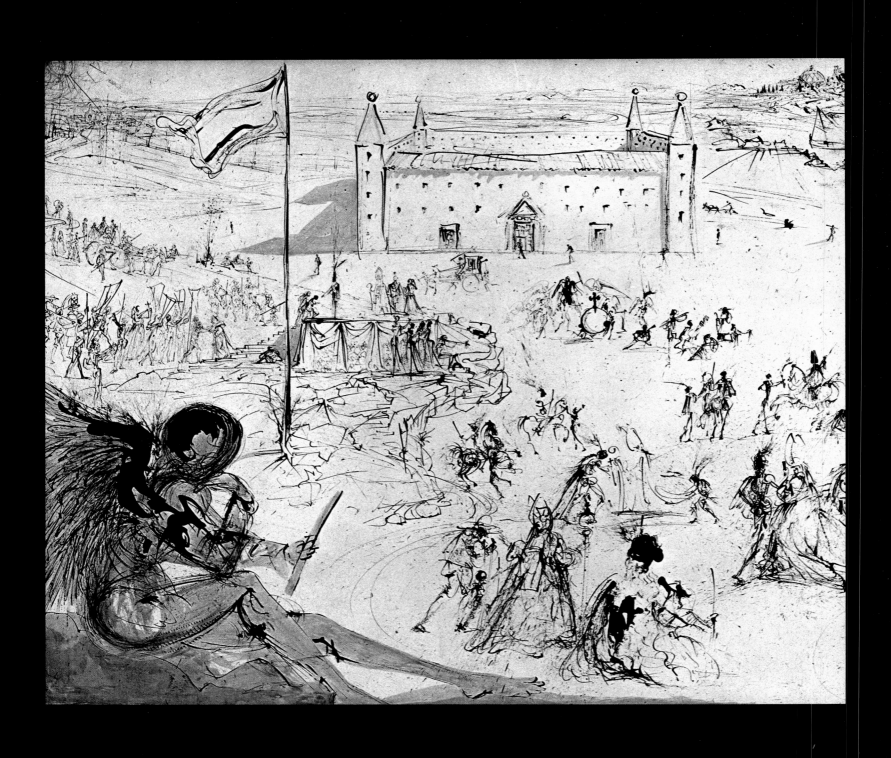

Tuna Fishing (1966–67), oil on canvas (304 × 404 cm / 119¾ × 159 in), Paul Ricard Foundation, Paris. Following pages: Details from this work. "The name must, so to speak, germinate or else it is false. The main contribution of surrealism to poetry as well as the plastic arts is to have exalted this germination enough to make everything that is not part of it appear derisory. As I was able to verify from a distance, the definition of surrealism given in the First Manifesto only revives one of the traditional rallying cries and which must thus 'burst the drum of reasoning reason and contemplate the hole,' which thus produces illuminating symbols that were hitherto obscure." (André Breton, *Du Surréalism dans ses oeuvres vivants.)*

Portrait of Gala (1969), ink drawing. Teatro Museo Dalí, Figueras. Following pages: *Ruggero Liberating Angelica* (1974), oil on canvas, Teatro Museo Dalí, Figueras. *Anchorite* (1974), oil on canvas, Teatro Museo Dalí, Figueras. *Figure Seen from Behind* (1974), gouache, Teatro Museo Dalí, Figueras. Dalí assigns the best part to woman at every level, poetry, images, and existence. According to Goethe, she incarnates the highest and most sublime possibilities of mankind. Surrealism mediates from romanticism this concept to put on trial, not without quite insurmountable obstacles, the so-called dualism of body and soul, not forgetting at least that "there is nothing in life that can prevail against the thirst that we get from it" (Breton).

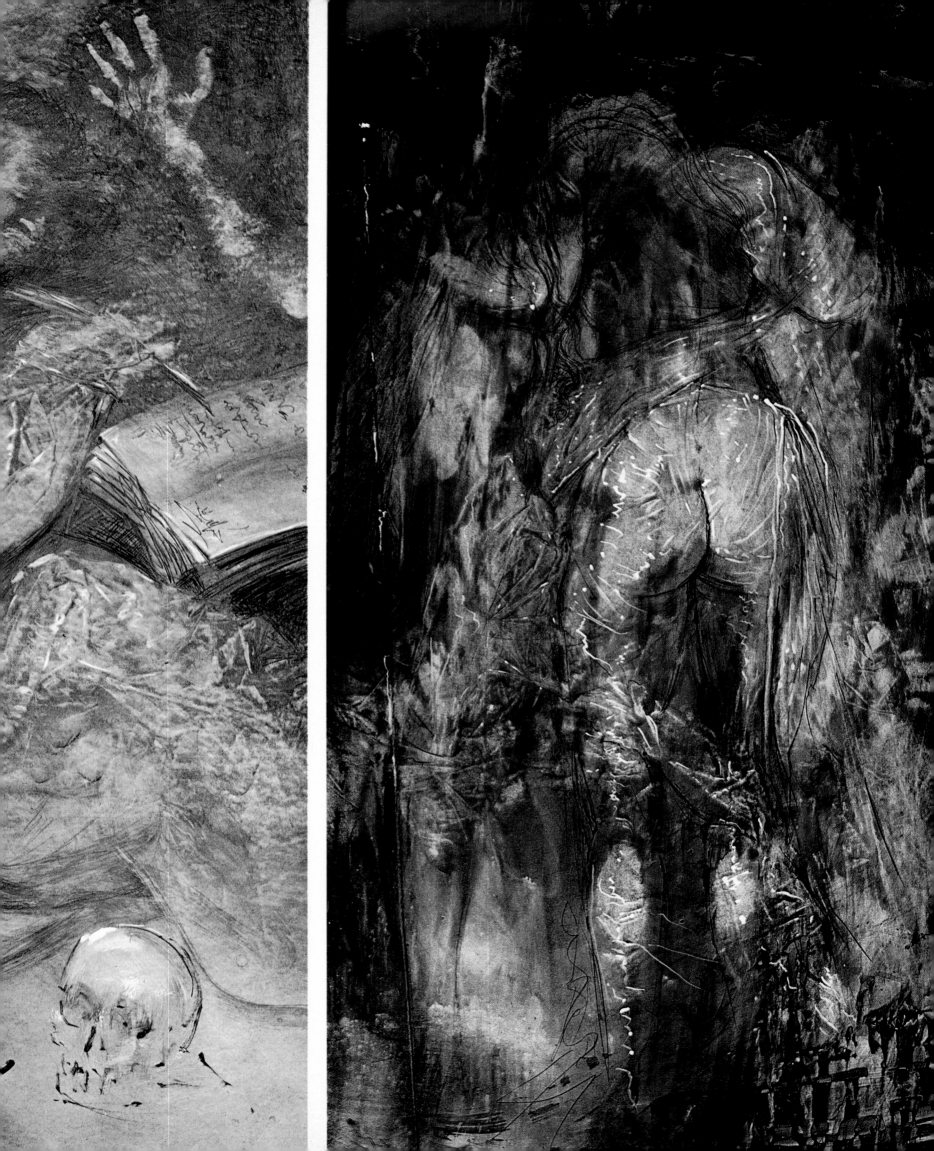

Explosion of Faith in a Cathedral (1974), oil on canvas, Teatro Museo Dalí, Figueras. Following pages: Detail from this painting. *Angels Watching the Ordination of a Saint* (1974), pen and ink, Teatro Museo Dalí, Figueras. Dali said, "Throughout my life it has in fact been very difficult for me to get used to the disconcerting and flabbergasting 'normality' of the beings who surround me and who people the world. I always say to myself, 'Nothing of what might happen ever happens!' I cannot understand why human beings should be so little individualized, why they should behave with such great collective uniformity. Take a simple thing as amusing oneself by derailing trains! Think of the thousands of kilometers of railroad tracks that cover the earth, in Europe, America and Asia!" Was "the explosion" something that "had to happen"?

Transformation (1974), oil on canvas, Teatro Museo Dalí, Figueras. Following pages: *Putrefied Bird* (circa 1928), oil on panel (375 × 57 cm / 14¾ × 22⅜), Teatro Museo Dalí, Figueras. *Nude Torso* (circa 1928), oil on panel (79.5 × 38.5 cm / 31⅜ × 15⅛ in), Teatro Museo Dalí, Figueras. The "coherent" argument against what appears as "logical reality" is surrealism, a reality just as logical to the point where just for this it was declared "in the service of the revolution." The consequence of this was that many mistakenly embraced communism with the deep disagreements and delusions that characterized the whole group. The liberty of surrealism was the antithesis of an imposition of socialist realism and anathemas from all sides condemned the "transformations" of so many of them.

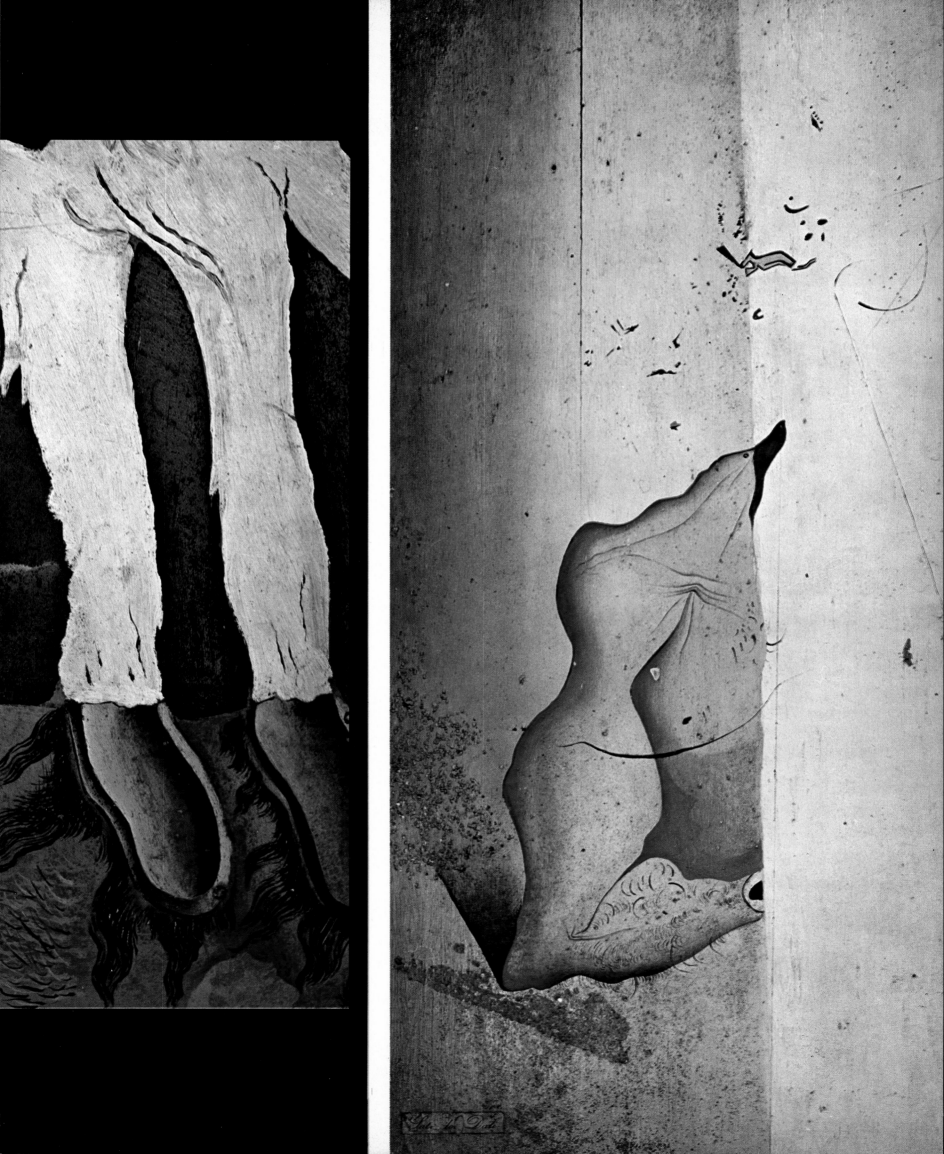

A Unique Setting
for a Unique Talent

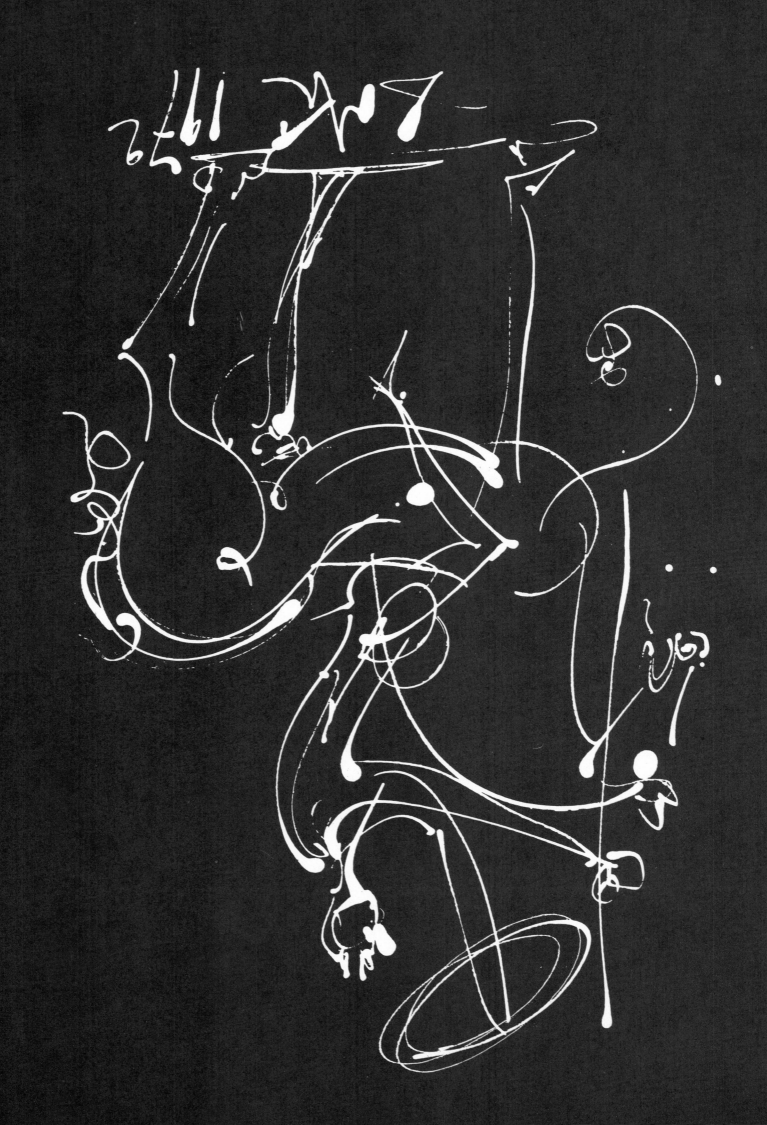

The Dalí Theater Museum at Figueras

Note by Eleonora Bairati

At twilight on September 28, 1974, in spite of driving rain and a freezing wind, a strange procession wound its way through the streets of Figueras, a little town in Catalonia where Salvador Domenech Felipe Jacinto Dalí was born on May 11, 1904. The procession consisted of groups in traditional costume, bands of majorettes, and even a little elephant that had somehow gotten involved as it wound its way to the town square, where the theater stood facing the church in which Dalí—who defined himself as "Catholic, apostolic, and Roman"—was baptized. In spite of its delightful appearance and unsophisticated spontaneity, this "happening" was somehow reminiscent of Dada and surrealist avant-garde activities, but it took place in fact to celebrate the foundation of the Teatro Museo Dalí, donated by this eccentric Catalán artist together with a large number of his works to his birthplace. Inside, the theater was packed with local and national dignitaries and photographers to see Dalí presented with the highest honours and gold medal of Figueras. He replied: "Our Caudillo has told me this museum will become the Mecca of contemporary art lovers. I would like it to be the spiritual center of Europe. From today this spiritual center is fixed on the perpendicular coming from the dome over the museum. Following the desires of Pérez Piñero, as they are my wishes too, I dedicate the dome to the Princes of Spain."

These significant words marked the latest act in Dalí's life-long publicity campaign for himself; as his sometime friend and enemy André Breton said, "He has an undeniable talent for presenting himself to the public." In his seventieth year and in the best of health, he inaugurated his museum-monument-sanctuary-tomb following the tradition of former Spanish kings, and with this in mind he had

One of the rooms in the Teatro Museo Dalí. The painter had experienced all the contradictions of his time, even those of daily life, with the perfect "coherence of incoherence," translated into what he himself has defined as "pop, op, yes, yes" art, which became "pompier." In this room of his museum tomb things are arranged to resemble one of his pictures, even the hair around the doorway.

himself photographed sitting on a gold throne under the royal crown carved on it and holding his famous scepter-cane—which may have belonged to Sarah Bernhardt—below a portrait of himself as a young man. So this extravagant act of self-celebration coincided with a kind of solemn and magnificent and typically Spanish ceremony, part of the ancient traditions of a country where life and death are inextricably entwined, and the reason for the Teatro Museo Dalí being founded at Figueras, halfway between the crypt of the Escorial and the sanctuary of the Valle de los Caídos. And at the time of the ceremony the interminable death agony of Francisco Franco had begun and was to be prolonged artificially with a macabre stink of putrefaction and holy water, until his death eventually came a year later, on November 20, 1975. Perhaps the Teatro Museo Dalí is the last mausoleum of the old Spain.

Dalí's life has always shown that his personal mythology is linked with certain places: Figueras, the village of Cadaqués on the coast, and the sea at Port Lligat, where he had his sanctuary. The process of solemnizing this house at Port Lligat has been continual, vibrant, dynamic, and full of the ups and downs of real life. The house has grown from the cottage acquired by Dalí and Gala in 1930 and like a living organism has produced new cells by gemmation to extend the life of the body. It is highly significant that just when the house finished growing and took on its final shape Gala added in 1961 the Egg Room, the final cell, an egg-shaped room dedicated to the myth of Leda (identifiable with Gala herself), and to the egg itself, which has since ancient times been the symbol of life and eternity. The theater museum was first planned in 1961 as a memorial to Dalí, built in his own lifetime.

In fact his initial plan for the museum was in itself brilliant. The municipal theater at Figueras was an ideal choice. An elegant early-nineteenth-century neoclassical building, it had been hit by incendiary bombs during the Civil War, and the roof of the central auditorium was completely destroyed, so it was used as a bivouac for Franco's Moroccan troops. Dalí first wanted to use it as it

Other views of the room shown on the previous page.

was, making the first "ready-made museum," almost in honour of the surrealist origins he had turned his back on, where works of art would be displayed in the stark holes torn in the walls by the bombs and the ruins left untouched. It was a very original idea, but too difficult to put into practice, so finally the museum took a quite different shape in the hands of Dalí and the architect Emilio Pérez Piñero. At first they wanted to make a reticular structure with a metal framework based on the cube. "This veritable curtain of sliding windows that fold back on each other is based on *Discourses on the Cube* by Juan de Herrera, who built the Escorial under Philip II. Thanks to this the old Figueras theater is to become a kinetic Sainte-Chapelle."

With his usual amazing ability to absorb every technical and artistic detail of a trend likely to catch on, Dalí made the museum a treasury of prefabricated modular structures and kinetic experiments. However, it was still no more than a project for a mobile and open building. The next plans were more definite: the great hole left by the bombs was to be covered with a geodesic dome inspired by the famous domes of Buckminster Fuller, and this made the building far more akin to a mausoleum. From ancient times a dome has always had an explicit symbolical significance—it is divine because it represents the sky, and it is thus a symbol of both human and divine authority: it covers both altars and tombs of kings. Dalí said that the dome is "an eminently monarchic principal, vital, and liturgical," with which the official sanctifying of the museum-tomb was complete.

It must be understood that the choice of a dome, which is a traditional architectural feature is not retrogressive in itself, since the official world cohabits with its own traditions to find the answers to its history and to change the present and plan for the future. The controversial and complex relationship between art, science, and technology so typical of the modern world is not reactionary in itself. These are ways in which Dalí justifies using these elements, which thus have a negative value, since the celebration of the restoration of the Spanish monarchy in itself justifies the return to the dome (spherical architecture as a sort of absolute monarchy) and the inspiration gained from Buckminster Fuller, "great monarchist architect," by Piñero, "the greatest architect of the monarchy."

Dalí's attitude towards architecture must be seen in this light. He was the first, at an earlier date, to value the great Catalán architect Antonio Gaudí for his contribution to that current that runs from Juan de Herrera to Emilio Pérez Piñero, the two "monarchist" architects, a current he discerns with an iconoclastic indifference which enabled him to say, "Le Corbusier has committed a terrible error: they will never use reinforced concrete on other planets. Le Corbu, Le Corbi, Le Corbo, Le Corbeau, Le Corbogre, Le Corbeau-de-malheur, Le Corbeau-mort, Le Corbusier has drowned. Yes, yes, and yes: he has fallen straight down under the weight of his reinforced-concrete Swiss, protestant, and masochistic cheese. On the structural plane Cézanne is like Le Corbusier, the only difference between them stemming from the fact that Cézanne was an angry reactionary full of good intentions, while Le Corbusier was unremittingly Swiss, progressive and full of bad intentions. Piñero, though, is an authentic Spanish genius: he has created the sublime dome of the Teatro Museo Dalí at Figueras because, like Fuller, he is able to bring to life molecular structures with deoxyribonucleic acid, the eternal factor."

Dalí is a unique equation in the history of modern art, which makes the avant-garde seem so reactionary; we should really be thinking that all he produced in the last ten years is the only last, supreme, and possible act of Dada, a total acceptance of "kitsch."

The Teatro Museo Dalí is a proof of this—a place to house collections of objects in accordance with a museum's traditional function, and as such an object itself—a "kitsch" object, both repulsive and gripping, which has progressed from an obviously pop-art and op-art style, to what Dalí has so cleverly and provocatively called "art pompier," the actual resting place of modern art according to the great artist of Figueras. Surely the Theatro Museo Dalí is the only authentic example of this art in existence.

One of the works in the Teatro Museo Dalí, opened in 1974 in the painter's birthplace with the participation of many different people from Catalonia, popular and traditional groups, giants and dwarfs, authorities and majorettes from Montpellier and Figueras.

"Furnishings" from a room in the
Teatro Museo Dalí (above).
Below, Dalí seated on a gold
throne carved with a crown and
holding his famous scepter-stick
on the day of the inauguration of
the museum. Right, a bust in the
museum, Homage to Diego
Velázquez.

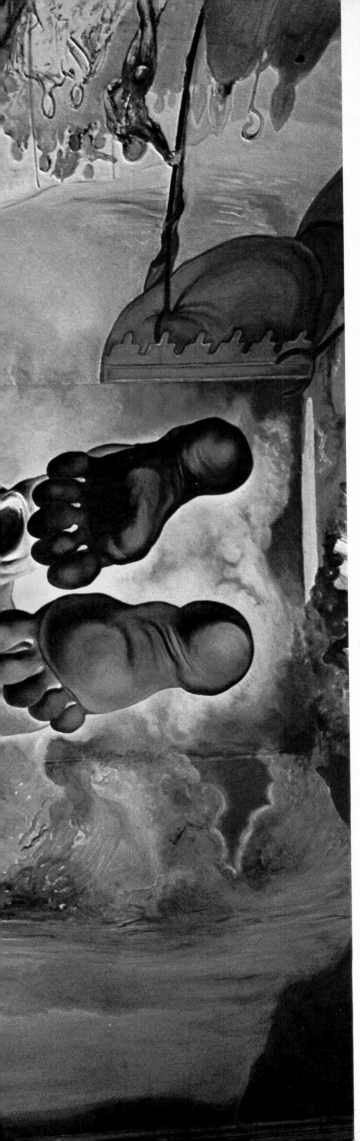

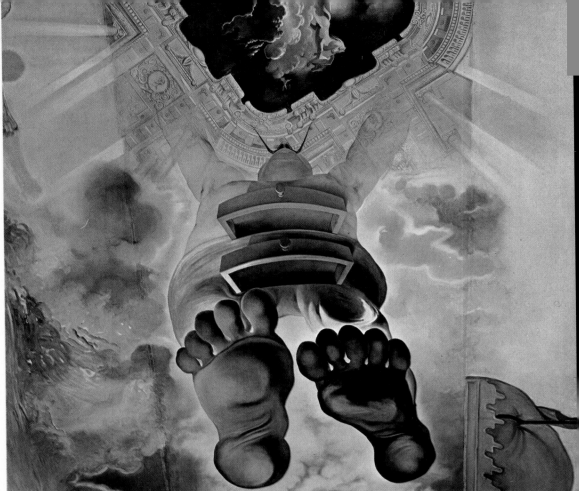

Details from the frescoes on the foyer ceiling. Dali with "inverted drawers" reaching up with Gala towards that highly personal form of mysticism of the painter that "recalls the railway station at Perpignan." His stiff moustaches point the way like antennae—as he calls them himself.

199

The foyer in the Teatro Museo, details of which are shown on the previous page. This foyer contains Homage to Velázquez, *one of Dalí's favourite artists, about whom he said, "If you told me a Velázquez had been born in Finland I would not even go and see him" and "I will paint Velázquez's* Las Meninas *in glorious colours."*

Other works exhibited in the Teatro Museo Dalí and views of the different rooms (also on the following pages). The day it was opened the artist received a gold medal from the city of Figueras from the mayor, while his wife gave Gala some flowers.

202

SE RUEGA
NO TOCAR

The geodesic dome above the hall of the Teatro Museo Dalí, which was the old eighteenth-century theater of Figueras, destroyed by bombing in the Civil War. It was in fact first a convent, then a Romantic theater. Right: Chair-picture-sculpture with a special conception of perspective.

Detail of the main room in the Teatro Museo Dalí, below the dome. Left: one of the paintings. The "reconstruction" of the theater museum was carried out by Dalí and the architect Emilio Pérez Piñero: his "reticular spatial structure generated by the cube" is based on the theories of Juan de Herrera, who built the Escorial.

Other details of the main room that lies below the dome (and on following pages). The dome copies molecular structures and was inspired by the work of the architect Buckminster Fuller, especially the Biosphere of the 1967 Universal and International Exposition in Montreal. One wall recalls the paintings of cypresses and sky Dali used to decorate the walls of the ducal palace in Milan after the ceiling was destroyed by bombing in the war, for his exhibition right after the end of the war.

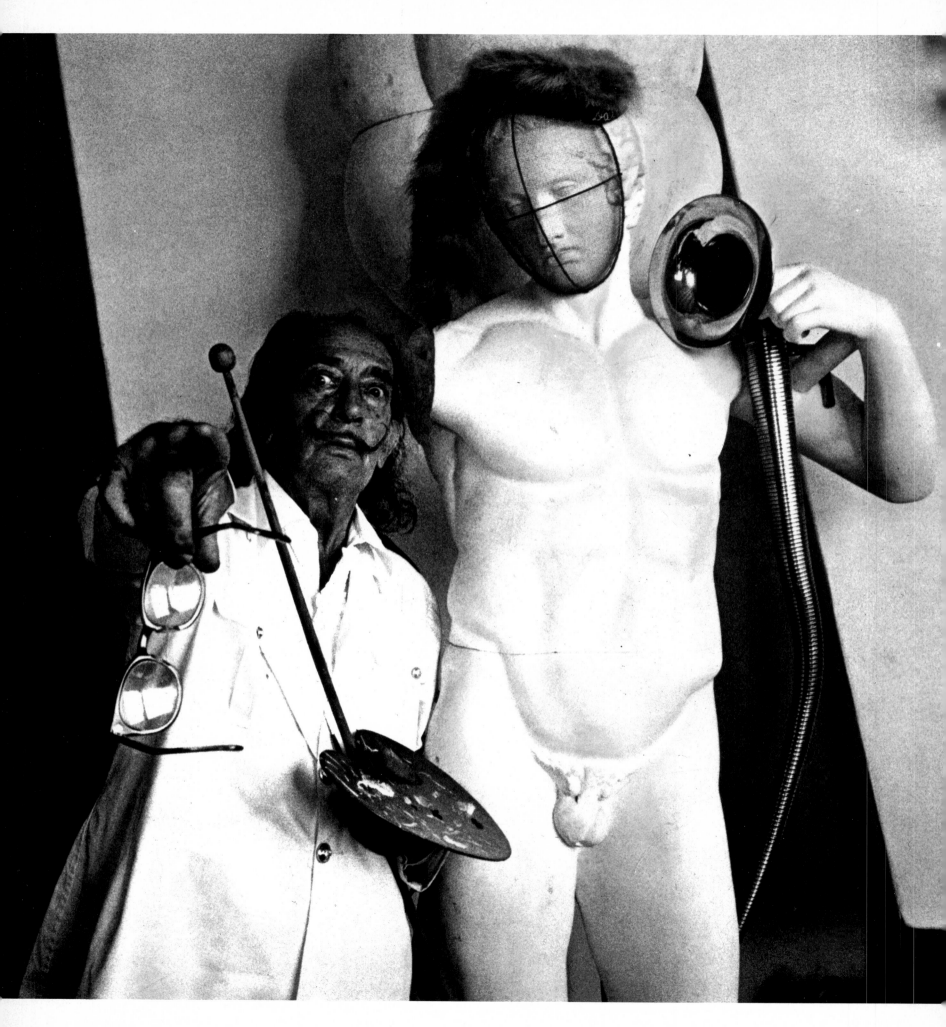

Inventiveness—the Key to Survival

An Interview with Dalí by Baltasar Porcel

Decadent and petrific, phantasmagorical and keenly provocative—these are some of the words which might be applied to the Theater Museum of Salvador Dalí. It stands in the painter's native village of Figueras, in the province of Ampurdán, bathed in the frigid luminosity of northern Spain against the jagged calligraphy of the Pyrenees.

The north winds whistle across the vast expanse of roof, which is bathed in an ashen light.

In the gloom of the night, the building still echoes with the nasal chants of the monks which the building once housed, but even more with bursts of laughter and applause, evocative of lascivious glances at opulent décolletés, from the romantic, bourgeois, pompous theater which federal Figueras built here in the middle of the nineteenth century.

But in this country of ours with its enthusiasms and devastations, a century is not a hundred years. The Civil War brought a bomb which laid open the roof and the victorious Moors, the *franquistas,* with their pathetic, muddled smiles, camped on the deserted stage, keeping warm around a fire of dismembered chairs and torn-up programs. In February 1939 it was the turn of the building itself; a crackling blaze engulfed the theater, leaving the blackened ruins exposed to progressive and solitary corrosion until in 1961 Salvador Dalí had the idea of rescuing them, of converting them into a spectacle and a memorial to his genius and ingenuity, of his alienation and his art, of his extravagance and his calculation.

"That's right; it was in 1961 when, looking one day at those tremendous ruins, I had the idea of the theater museum. Where, if not in my own town, would I put the most extravagant and most durable of my works? The Municipal Theater, or what remained of it, seemed to me ideally suited, for three reasons: first, because I am an eminently theatrical painter; second, because the theater stands in front of the church in which I was baptized—and, as you well know, Porcel, I am a Catholic, both apostolic and Roman; and third, because it was in the foyer of that very theater that I first exhibited my painting."

"Are you a sentimentalist?"

"No, a racialist. And full of dazzling subterranean passages—for the idea of this theater museum originated much earlier, in 1945, when a major exhibition of my work was held in another bombed-out building, in the magnificent hall of the Caryatids in the old Royal Palace in Milan. They had blanked off the great ceiling in a bland gesture of defiance to the sculptured, eighteenth-century decoration of the immense room, and it seemed as though the latter did not have a ceiling, that that colourless surface was the sky. I painted a few cypresses on it, as if they were planted outside, which in reality they were. I converted one reality into another, which in its turn gave rise to another: this theater museum, which we inaugurated in September 1974."

We walk through the rooms. Dalí seems to be looking and yet not looking. There are visitors looking at paintings, objects, spaces, half admiring, half bewildered. Dalí, slightly stooping, adorned with his fearsome moustache, continues his Dalinian peroration.

"Even if it did not contain a single work of mine people would immediately realize on entering that they are in a Dalinian sidereal space. My genius is unlimited in scope, and painting is only a small part of it."

"Nevertheless, people say that you have given very little of your work to the museum—"

"It's a lie, on the third floor there is a whole heap of paintings, drawings, sculpture, engravings, which give an idea of my whole career. And between Paris and New York, Gala and I have a hundred tremendous works to give to the theater museum. But we are administering them with a medicine dropper, one by one, because if you give everything at once no one will thank you for it. This way, giving them slowly, people appreciate them. Señor Barona, who lived in Figueras, about whom I am writing a book which will be a collection of philosophical anecdotes, said one day to some football players who went to complain to him about something or other: 'Don't worry, leave it all to me, and then no one will be able to complain without a reason.' " Dalí laughs.

There is something in the atmosphere, a mixture of the habitual and the unfamiliar, which reminds me of the expostulations of Ramón Gómez de la Serna, of his prolific output of domesticated, poetic surrealism.

"It seems to me, Don Salvador, that in some of these corners one can catch a glimpse of the square face, the impertinent bow tie, the flat pipe of R—"

"Yes, Ramón Gómez de la Serna. When I really got to

215

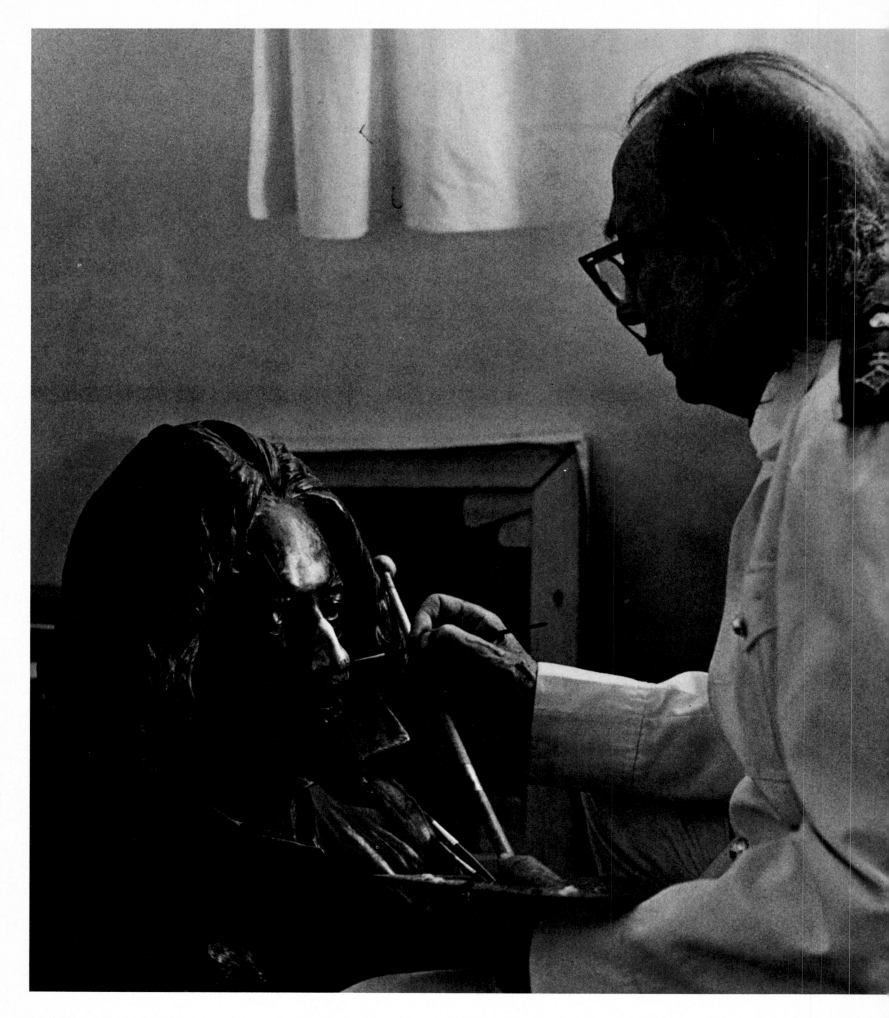

Dalí working in the studio of his house at Port Lligat and a view of Port Lligat. It was a fisherman's cottage given to Gala by the widow Lidia Sabana de Costa.

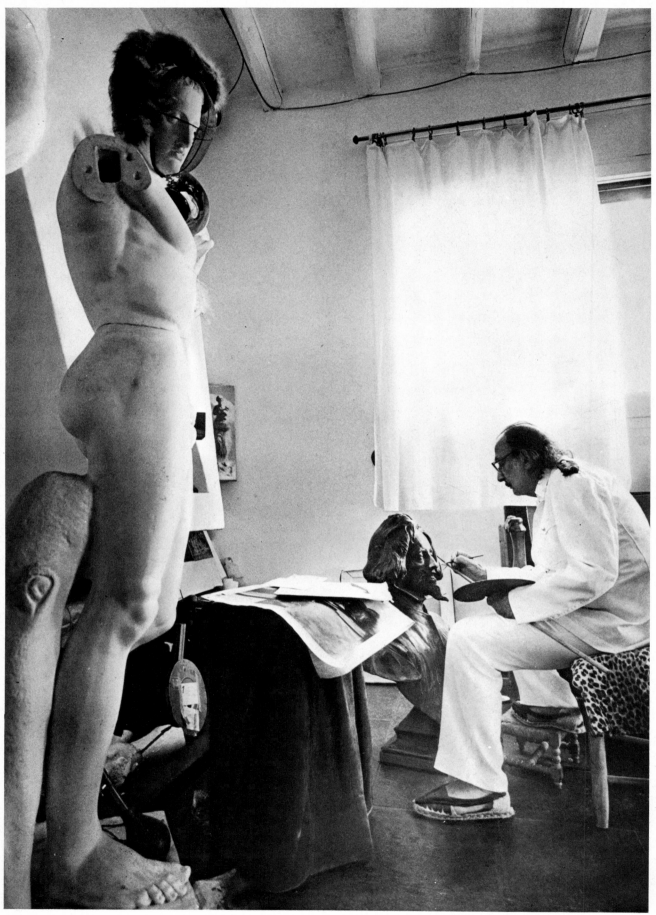

Other aspects of Dalí's life: above, and right with his scepter-stick in the house at Port Lligat, which he calls "my spiritual prison." The original cottage was extended by buying adjoining sheds, and doorways were made between them.

know him, I realized that he was far superior to all that stuff he used to churn out, though it's now in a very good series. He is one of the most important Spanish writers of that period, or the '98, as it's now called, don't you think?"

"Well, up to a point . . ."

"Above all, he's an extraordinarily solid and sustained writer. Without a shadow of doubt. And there are moments when he attains real genius, particularly when he's talking about a shop which there was in Madrid, in which Velázquez's painting *The Spinning Women* [*Las Hilanderas*] was reproduced in the window, with all its different shades of codfish: that light ochre, the greenish colour . . . Gómez de la Serna makes it into a sublime piece of literature. But obviously there's no comparison with our deceased friend Josep María de Sagazza, whose verses sometimes achieved greater quantity than quality. Like mine. A biological secretion."

"And what do you think of the text of that book which he wrote about you before he died?"

"The fact is that Gómez de la Serna did not know me personally very well. But even so there are three or four insights about my painting in it which no one else has had. And that is fundamental. If he had lived, Gómez de la Serna would have ended up a metaphysical monarch like me, and then indeed the book about me would have had no equal."

High above us, as if calling us towards the necessarily incomplete regions of some spatial dream, the jointed, geodesic dome of the architect Piñero reigns over us, over Figueras.

"Would you say that you and Gómez de la Serna are linked by the umbilical cord of surrealism?"

"Yes, of course, of course. But surrealism, bah! . . . The important thing is to live and work, and then to think. Surrealism succeeded in doing the contrary: it practiced a false automatism, a calculated operation, a programming of the unprogrammable. I am above all that. I live and then I do. For example, let me show you this, which I did today—a building. You see this photograph—a house with eyes for windows which close and open like eyelashes. It is based on an advertisement: I saw it this morning, while I was reading the newspaper in bed. I cut it out, added the extra bit at the side, and used the caption as the front steps, simply and graphically, like that, you see? The eyes would have to be hyperrealistic, transparent—it would make a nice little house, don't you think? The difference between my ideas and those of others is that others may have a dream which vanishes, while with my paranoiac-critical activity the dream may be turned into a building of stone, or of cement, if you prefer it."

I am at a loss for an answer, and Dalí is quick to notice it.

"Don't start talking to me about taste. About good taste. Oh, no! Bad taste is the most creative thing there is. Or rather, it overcomes everything else. Take Gaudí, for instance. With him there's no question of taste, just a crea-

219

tive power which inundates everything, overwhelms it. So-called good taste weakens the creative force. I suppose you noticed that this house I invented is soft, encephalic, like Gaudí's architecture. Quite the opposite of that monster Le Corbusier, who had to recant in the end. He used to say that buildings were "machines for living." When we met, he remarked to me: "You're a man who has lots of ideas. What do you think the architecture of the future will be like?" "Soft," I replied. "How's that?" "Like what Gaudí produced," I said, and putting his hands on his head he replied, "Gaudí is the shame of Barcelona." I have always been the great defender of Gaudí. Others came later and defended him too, and it is they who are credited with his rehabilitation. It's always the same with me. I'm the one who makes the discovery, the first in the field, and the one who gets robbed. I once said to Coco Chanel: 'Ideas are thought up in order to be stolen.' They can steal what they like from me. I don't know what would become of me without my extraordinary, fabulous capacity for invention, which enables me to survive in spite of everything."

"Exactly, Señor Dalí. And now that we have started to talk about painting—"

"Oh, painters! They're a lot of donkeys. I prefer to deal with philosophers or, even better, with scientists."

"But you, Señor Dalí, must know you're a great painter, and no donkey."

"I'm like all the rest. I have the brain of a genius, and I say it in all sincerity. But as a painter I'm a disaster. Look at Velásquez, for example—there's an extraordinary painter. I may be the best painter living today, but that's a very different matter. They are all extremely bad. Look at Chagall, for instance. If history says of me that I was the best painter in the province of Gerona, I shall be satisfied."

"Well, I must say, Señor Dalí, that Velásquez doesn't excite me. If I had to choose, I think I would opt for a Turner."

"Turner? He's the worst painter in the world. He tries to produce a luminous effect and comes out with a fucking pastel. There aren't any good English painters. All the Spaniards are good, on the other hand. Painting is a question of what country one comes from. For example, Miró and Tapiés are two fabulous painters. But if the tendency which they follow were adopted by some Finns, the result would be horrible. Both races have an extraordinary quality of their own. You can tell them a mile off. If you told me that a Velásquez had been produced in Finland, I wouldn't even go to see it. In that country it would be impossible."

Against the fantastic Gothic *cum* cultural *cum* geodesic background stands the gigantic figure of Queen Esther, a monument to physical plenitude and expressiveness, sculpted by Ernst Fuchs.

"Five years ago, Señor Dalí, you were very rude about Joan Miró, as I recorded in my book *La Palabra del arte.*"

"Was I really? Well, I shouldn't have been. He's a mag-nificent painter."

"I agree entirely, Señor Dalí."

"But Richard Estes, the hyperrealist, is even better. Seriously, as far as I'm concerned he's the best in the world. He works methodically, incessantly, polishing his colour tones, refining the drawing, making his paintings more and more like a photograph. As I shall never tire of saying, photography has been the salvation of painting. It's reality exalted, exacerbated! Take structuralism—it was claimed to be the great discovery of our time, but it merely dissects, without seeking a new structure. It's like impressionism, in which everything was fleeting, insubstantial, because it lacked an axis, something inside. With hyperrealism you can see if you're making progress, if you're perfecting your art. But how do you know it if you're painting abstract? There everything is the same."

"What have you got to say about Picasso?"

"People were always trying to oppose us, but that was wrong. Dalí is the only painter with whom Picasso wanted to cooperate. That's been proved now, because they have found an engraving, the original of which we did together. I put in some fried eggs and passed it to him. He added a chair, then passed it back to me. I drew him an ironing board, and so on. Picasso was a communist, you know. But that's irrelevant when it comes to painting badly or well, for I insist that painting is something racial. Think of Russia. There are some marvellous writers—Dostoyevsky, for instance; the composers and musicians are sublime; but there are no painters, and it's not just because of socialist realism. Velásquez's *Las Lanzas* was a perfect piece of historical realism. You may find a great painting of the Battle of Stalingrad. But the fact is that Russia is not a country of painters. There's not a single one. And in France there are third-rate masters like Bouguereau. The best is Millet with his *Angelus.* Much better than Cézanne. I've always maintained it and now it's being proved true ... But that's enough old history. The important thing about Dalí is that he invented hyperrealist painting before the rest of the world had even imagined it. He prophesied it, in the middle of the abstract movement. Everyone laughed: 'No one will ever draw a nose again.' And now what do we have—in New York there's nothing but hyperrealism."

Dalí keeps twirling his stick like a windmill; he claims it belonged to Sarah Bernhardt. He irreverently thumps the radiant staircase by the Rumanian Damián which leads to the former stage, to the whole Theater Museum, to the theater of Daliism.

"Señor Dalí, which of your pictorial phases do you think will prove most lasting?"

"Undoubtedly the one I've just announced in a flurry of ballyhoo—metaphysical hyperrealism. Now I'm making a hole in the horizon and beginning to paint things right on that horizon. And everything there is behind the horizon is metaphysical. And it has to be looked at through a stereoscope. We've reached the metaphysics of de Chirico, which I'm resolving through pure mathematics. Here, put

One of the rooms in Dalí's house at Port Lligat and a detail of the same room. The most famous are the throne rooms, the snail room, and the last "additional cell"—the egg room—all Gala's own work.

on these lenses and look through them at these two little watercolours, which are apparently the same. You see how the perspective stands out? There are clouds, the horizon is blue and beyond it, you can see some wash basins hanging in the air, and then out into space, towards the infinite, where I shall paint Velásquez's *Las Meninas* in glorious colours."

"You're very clever, Señor Dalí."

"What do you want me to say? Perhaps too clever . . . So you see, you're witnessing something which has never been done before—a single painter painting a single painting which is two paintings at the same time, so that each can be looked at by one of the two eyes which everyone has. Later these watercolours will be an enormous canvas which will be exhibited in the Guggenheim in New York, where you've already seen that other big canvas of mine which is either Gala or Lincoln according to how one looks at it."

"And what do you think of these works, Señor Dalí? Are they outstanding?"

"I don't care a damn. The thing which matters is the experiment. All the rest can be shit, it doesn't matter. Anyway, this only took me a moment. I did it here in the hotel. And there's more. Did you know that a museum of holography has been set up in New York? Do you know what holography is? It's nothing more or less than the combination of hyperrealism and metaphysics, brought about by interference in the coherent light called laser. If you break up a hologram into an infinite number of pieces, each piece contains a complete record of the image engraved on the emulsion of the hologram. In other words, we're experiencing the combination of science and art.

From Outer Mongolia to Alexandrines

Now we come to Dalí's own paintings, displayed in all their fascination: *The Church of Cadaqués, from Port Al-*

221

guer, *at Eight O'Clock in the Morning,* the *Léda Atomica, The Bread Basket, The Specter of Desire* . . . surrealism, hyperrealism, always a suggestive combination of mystery and reality.

"In this view, Señor Dalí, the painting—"

"You're too fond of painting. Ask me about something more important, like *Impressions of Outer Mongolia.*"

"Very well, Don Salvador, what about *Impressions of Outer Mongolia?*"

"I'll tell you. It's a film which was made by some Germans who came to my hotel in New York, the St. Regis-Sheraton, to take some film of me. I'm always on the boil, and at the time I was having an extraordinary experience. I had gone to urinate in the lavatory in the hotel, and there I found a white fountain pen with a metal cap which had been lying in the urinal for some time and was half corroded by the uric acid. I said to the Germans, you ought to film that, just focus on the pen, which I'll keep turning slowly, and record my voice, what I'm saying. They set to work. When this is shown on a screen, one sees fabulous lunar landscapes, strange, bearded, and magical, and you hear me describing them in exact detail: lakes, mountains, passes. You can see Outer Mongolia. It's better than my other films, including *Le Chien andalou,* which I made with Buñuel almost half a century ago."

"And you write too, Señor Dalí."

"My father said I was a better painter than a writer, and he was right. I've published about thirty books. I'm writing one now, it's there on the piano—a tragedy in the style of Corneille, in Alexandrines, which I've been working on for six years."

"I didn't know you could write verse, Don Salvador."

"Well, I'm learning at the moment . . . But the tragedy will be a work of genius, like everything I do. It's called *Martyr* and it takes place in Holland in that period. And it's a heresy, a revolt against original sin. The protagonist does not admit it, and wants to return to Lilith, Adam's first wife before Eve, and wants to resuscitate Rome. There are three characters. In the first act everyone thinks that the martyr is her; in the second that it is the prince, who wants to marry her; but in the third act it turns out to be the priest, who upholds respect for the law. I do the opposite of what they did in Racine's time, when there was a tendency to assume that might is right."

"You're a rebel, Don Salvador. Now let's take a hyperrealist jump and talk about the oil crisis. What do you think of it—could you resolve it, could you deal with the multinationals and the oil sheiks?"

"I'm not in the least bit interested, it's mere supposition. It's as if we were talking about women and you suddenly wanted to talk about Gala, the sublime Gala."

Final Apotheosis with Gala and Catalonia

"Gala. Who is Gala? When I first met her in Paris, she hardly seemed a separate person from the one I had seen in hundreds of paintings and drawings, frozen in time, converted into a concept by Salvador Dalí."

"What about this whole story of you and Gala, Señor Dalí? Does it correspond to reality, did she really have such an influence over you, or is it pure fiction?"

"It's reality. She transformed me. Without Gala, Dalí would be as much of a genius as he is, but he would be living in a hovel full of lice and candle drippings. He would be a disaster, half mad, half an illuminate. It was she who brought me out, introduced me to a life of triumph. Her first husband, the poet Paul Eluard, described her marvellously when he said that she had eyes which could penetrate walls. I get taken in by everyone. But if she was here, she would know at a glance who is good and who is a scoundrel."

"On another subject, Señor Dalí, you have the reputation of not being very fond of what we call Catalonia. One might even call you an anti-Catalán—"

"It's a lie. I'm more pro-Catalán than anyone. I'm against some Catalán intellectuals, because sometimes, with all due respect, they're asses; they're asses because they don't read Francesc Pujols, the greatest philosopher in Spain, whose work contains the whole of Catalán philosophy. I've had him translated into Spanish, and French, and I read him every night. His memory shines in me like the sun. Listen to this passage by him: 'And if anyone is surprised that a people like that of Catalonia, which beside other nations is nothing and represents nothing, because it has no political independence, which is the least that any people can possess, and carries no weight in the council of states, although Catalán views are always significant because they are full of reality—if anyone is surprised that such a nation could succeed in dominating the world without arms, we will reply to them that if when the Romans, *in illo tempore,* as the Latins said, were intent on dominating Judea, someone had told them that the day would come when the Jews would dominate them and the whole of Europe and almost the whole of America, which had not even been discovered then, we are as sure as if we could see it now, that they would have burst out laughing . . .' Eh? You're laughing!"

"Yes, Don Salvador."

"You're laughing at Pujols, like all the rest. A lot of donkeys. And you're wrong. Catalonia, the mystical and hyperrealist, has to dominate Castille, Spain, the world. And we will reach a golden age of metaphysics, as Pujols has already said: 'The day will come when we, the Catalúns, will have everything paid for, just because we're Cat-

The bear given to Dali by one of the greatest collectors of his work (Edward James), which the artist proposes to paint green to hide its age and discolouration. The house at Port Lligat "has grown like a biological structure by gemmation," according to a progression of Lidia delirious-paranoiac, Dali blastoforus, Gala divine protein (Galadeoxyribonucleic acid).

aláns—hotels, food, the lot.' What do you think of that?"

What does it matter what I think? Dalí is also, and even primarily, a monologuist. Dialogue hardly exists for him. Gómez de la Serna contributed an essay for this volume and one can imagine him pulling at his pipe as he wrote it: "Dalí's great instinct is for preserving his infantile impressions intact, with all their insights; he is quick to seize, and to release, the things which attract him, faster and franker than anyone to the minute, five thousand revolutions of times more than anyone else."

We have stopped in the central room of the old—the new?—theater. In the ceiling is a spectacular representation of Dalí, his whole figure a piece of furniture in which there are open drawers pouring out gold coins. Dalí points upwards with his cane. His eyes flash, his voice swells as he recites solemnly:

"Yes, it's like in the Middle Ages, mysticism and gold, truth and the philosopher's stone go hand in hand. I'm a mystic because I love money. And I am generous because every symbol is eternal and therefore given to humanity. As you have recorded in this book, Gómez de la Serna, when he was told that I had become commercialized, said, 'It's not true . . . commerce has come to Dalí, the dealers have been Dalified.' Look at those drawers, they keep opening and showering onto people, onto the public, all the money which I have extracted from them during my life. I'm returning from where I started. I'm merging with the gold and the people, with the earth and mysticism. Oh, yes, I'm a marvellous actor!"

Baltasar Porcel
Vallvidrera, February 1977

Testimonies

DALÍ ON HIMSELF

His love for Gala

Eluard's wife, Gala, struck me as having a very intelligent face.... She was destined to be my Gradiva, "she who advances," my victory, my wife!...

She was dressed in white on the day we had finally set. It was a very light dress that trembled so shudderingly as we climbed up the slope that she "made me cold." The wind became too violent as we went up, and I used this as a pretext for turning our walk away from the heights.

We climbed down again and went and sat down facing the sea on a slate bench cut into the rocks, which sheltered us from the slightest gust of wind. It was one of the most truculently deserted and mineral spots of Cadaqués, and the month of September held over us the "dying silver" garlic-clove of the incipient crescent moon, haloed by the primitive taste of tears that painfully knotted Gala's throat and mine. But we did not want to weep, we wanted to have it over with.

Gala's face wore a resolute expression.

"What do you want me to do to you?" I said to her, putting my arms around her.

She was speechless with emotion. She made several attempts to speak, and finally she shook her head abruptly, while tears flowed down her cheeks. I kept insisting. Then, with a decisive effort, she unsealed her lips at last to tell me, in a plaintive little child's voice,

"If you won't do it, you promise not to tell anyone?"

I kissed her on the mouth, inside her mouth. It was the first time I did this. I had not suspected until then that one could kiss in this way....

"What do you want me to do to you?"

Then Gala, transforming the last glimmer of her expression of pleasure into the hard light of her own tyranny, answered,

"I want you to kill me!"

No interpretation in the world could modify the meaning of this answer, which meant exactly what she said.

"Are you going to do it?" she asked.

I was so astonished and disappointed at having "my own secret" offered me as a present instead of the ardent erotic proposal I had expected that I was slow in answering her, lost in a whirl of undefinable perplexity.

"Are you going to do it?" I heard her repeat again.

Already the tone of her voice betrayed the disdain of doubt. I pulled myself together again, goaded by pride. I was suddenly afraid of destroying the faith Gala had had until then in my potentialities of moral courage and madness. Again I seized her in my arms, and in the most solemn manner of which I was capable I answered,

"YES!"

And I kissed her again, hard, on the mouth, while I repeated deep within myself, "No! I shall not kill her!"

And my second kiss to Gala, while it was a Judas kiss by virtue of the hypocrisy of my tenderness, simultaneously consummated the act of saving her life and resuscitated my own soul.

Against modern art

With the surrealist object I thus killed elementary surrealist painting, and modern painting in general. Miró had said, "I want to assassinate painting!" And he assassinated it—skillfully and slyly abetted by me, who was the one to give it its death-blow, fastening my matador sword between its shoulder-blades. But I do not think Miró quite realized that the painting that we were going to assassinate together was "modern painting." For I have just recently met the older painting at the opening of the Mellon collection, and I assure you it does not yet seem at all aware that anything untoward has happened to it.

At the height of the frenzy over surrealist objects I painted a few apparently very normal paintings, inspired by the congealed and minute enigma of certain snapshots, to which I added a Dalinian touch of Meissonier. I felt the public, which was beginning to grow weary of the continuous cult of strangeness, instantly nibble at the bait. Within myself I said, addressing the public, "I'll give it to you, I'll give you reality and classicism. Wait, wait a little, don't be afraid."

Meeting with America

In Paris, in fact, everyone judges things from the esthetic point of view of his own intellectual interests.... America was different....

America chooses with all the unfathomable and elementary force of her unique and intact biology. She knows, as does no one else, what she lacks, what she does not have. And all that America "did not have" on the spiritual plane I was going to bring her, materialized in the integral and delirious mixture of my paranoiac work, in order that she might thus see and touch everything with the hands of liberty. Yes, what America did not have was precisely the horror of my rotten donkeys from Spain, of the spectral aspect of the Christs of El Greco, of the whirling of the fiery sunflowers of Van Gogh, of the airy quality of Chanel's *décolletés,* of the oddness of fur cups, of the metaphysics of the surrealist manikins of Paris, of the apotheosis of the symphonic and Wagnerian architecture of Gaudí, of Rome, Toledo and Mediterranean Catholicism....

The idea I was beginning to form of America was corroborated by the impression produced upon me by a personal meeting with Alfred H. Barr, Jr., the director of the Museum of Modern Art of New York. I met him at a dinner at the Vicomte de Noailles'. He was young, pale, and very sickly-looking; he had stiff and rectilinear gestures like those of pecking birds—in reality he was pecking at contemporary values, and one felt that he had the knack of picking just the full grains, never the chaff. His information on the subject of modern art was enormous. By contrast with our European directors of modern museums, most of whom still had not heard of Picasso, Alfred Barr's erudition verged on the monstrous. Mrs. Barr, who spoke French, prophesied that I would have a dazzling future in America, and encouraged me to go there.

The break with Aragon and the disintegration of the surrealist group in Paris

I was no longer master of my legend, and henceforth surrealism was to be more and more identified with me, and with me only. Much water had passed under the bridge, and I found upon my return that the group I had known—both surrealists and society people—was in a state of complete disintegration. Preoccupations of a political nature had turned a great number of them toward the left, and a whole surrealist faction, obeying the slogans of Louis Aragon, a nervous little Robespierre, was rapidly evolving toward a complete acceptance of the communist cultural platform. This inner crisis of surrealism came to a head the day when, upon my suggesting the building of a "thinking-machine," consisting of a rocking chair from which would hang numerous goblets of warm milk, Aragon flared up with indignation. "Enough of Dalí's fantasies!" he exclaimed. "Warm milk for the children of the unemployed!"

Breton, thinking he saw a danger of obscurantism in the communist-sympathizing faction, decided to expel Aragon and his adherents—Buñuel, Unic, Sadoul, and others—from the surrealist group. I considered René Crevel the only completely sincere communist among those I knew at the time, yet he decided not to follow Aragon along what he termed "the path of intellectual mediocrity." Nevertheless he remained distant from our group, and shortly afterward committed suicide, despairing of the possibility of solving the dramatic contradictions of the ideological and intellectual problems confronting the postwar generation. Crevel was the third surrealist who committed suicide, thus corroborating their affirmative answer to a questionnaire that had been circulated in one of its first issues by the magazine *La Révolution Surréaliste,* in which it was asked, "Is suicide a solution?" I had answered no, supporting this negation with the affirmation of my ceaseless individual activity.

Enthusiasm for Renaissance art

Gala was beginning to interest me in a voyage to Italy. The architecture of the Renaissance, Palladio, and Bramante impressed me more and more as being the startling and perfect achievement of the human spirit in the realm of esthetics, and I was beginning to feel the desire to go and see and touch these unique phenomena, these products of materialized intelligence that were concrete, measurable and supremely nonnecessary. Also, Gala had decided to undertake some further building in our little house in Port Lligat—a new floor. She knew that this would distract me from my spells of anguish, and would canalize my attention on small immediate problems.

From day to day Gala was reviving my faith in myself. I would say, "It is impossible, even astrologically, to learn again, like the ancients, all the vestiges of technique that have disappeared. I no longer have time even to learn how to draw as they did before! I could never improve on the technique of a Boecklin!" Gala demonstrated to me by a thousand inspired arguments, burning with faith, that I could become something other than "the most famous surrealist" that I was. We were consumed with admiration over reproductions of Raphael. There one could find everything—everything that we surrealists have invented constituted in Raphael only a tiny fragment of his latent but conscious content of unsuspected, hidden, and manifest things. But all this was so complete, so synthetic, so "one," that for this very reason he eludes our contemporaries. The analytical and mechanical short-sightedness of the postwar period had in fact specialized in the thousand parts of which all "classic work" is composed, making of each part analyzed an end in itself which was erected as a banner to the exclusion of all the rest, and which was blasted forth like a cannon shot.

War had transformed men into savages. Their sensibility had become degraded. One could see only things that were terribly enlarged and unbalanced. After a long diet of nitroglycerine, everything that did not explode went unperceived. The metaphysical melancholy inherent in perspective could be understood only in the pamphleteering schemata of Chirico, when in reality this same sentiment was present, among a thousand other things, in Perugino, Raphael or Piero della Francesca. And in these painters, among a thousand other things, there were also to be found the problems of composition raised by cubism, etc., etc.; and from the point of view of sentiment—the sense of death, the sense of the libido materialized in each colored fragment, the sense of the instantaneity of the moral "commonplace"—what could one invent that Vermeer of Delft had not already lived with an optical hyperlucidity exceeding in objective poetry, in felt originality, the gigantic and metaphorical labor of all the poets combined! To be classic meant that there must be so much of "everything," and of everything so perfectly in place and hierarchically organized, that the

infinite parts of the work would be all the less visible. Classicism thus meant integration, synthesis, cosmogony, faith, instead of fragmentation, experimentation, skepticism.

From Salvador Dalí, The Secret Life of Salvador Dalí, *Dial Press,* New York, 1942.

THE BASIS OF SURREALISM

We are still living under the reign of logic: this, of course, is what I have been driving at. But in this day and age logical methods are applicable only to solving problems of secondary interest. The absolute rationalism that is still in vogue allows us to consider only facts relating directly to our experience. Logical ends, on the contrary, escape us. It is pointless to add that experience itself has found itself increasingly circumscribed. It paces back and forth in a cage from which it is more and more difficult to make it emerge. It too leans for support on what is most immediately expedient, and it is protected by the sentinels of common sense. Under the pretense of civilization and progress, we have managed to banish from the mind everything that may rightly or wrongly be termed superstition, or fancy; forbidden is any kind of search for truth which is not in conformance with accepted practices. It was, apparently, by pure chance that a part of our mental world which we pretended not to be concerned with any longer—and, in my opinion, by far the most important part—has been brought back to light. For this we must give thanks to the discoveries of Sigmund Freud. On the basis of these discoveries a current of opinion is finally forming by means of which the human explorer will be able to carry his investigations much further, authorized as he will henceforth be not to confine himself solely to the most summary realities. The imagination is perhaps on the point of reasserting itself, of reclaiming its rights. If the depths of our mind contain within it strange forces capable of augmenting those on the surface, or of waging a victorious battle against them, there is every reason to seize them—first to seize them, then, if need be, to submit them to the control of our reason. The analysts themselves have everything to gain by it. But it is worth noting that no means has been designated *a priori* for carrying out this undertaking, that until further notice it can be construed to be the province of poets as well as scholars, and that its success is not dependent upon the more or less capricious paths that will be followed. . . .

Surrealism does not allow those who devote themselves to it to forsake it whenever they like. There is every reason to believe that it acts on the mind very much as drugs do; like drugs, it creates a certain state of need and can push man to frightful revolts. It also is, if you like, an artificial paradise, and the taste one has for it derives from Baudelaire's criticism for the same reason as the others. Thus the analysis of the mysterious effects and special pleasures it can produce—in many respects surrealism occurs as a *new vice* which does not necessarily seem to be restricted to the happy few; like hashish, it has the ability to satisfy all manner of tastes—such an analysis has to be included in the present study.

1. It is true of surrealist images as it is of opium images that man does not evoke them; rather they "come to him spontaneously, despotically. He cannot chase them away; for the will is powerless now and no longer controls the faculties." It remains to be seen whether images have ever been "evoked." If one accepts, as I do, Reverdy's definition it does not seem possible to bring together, voluntarily, what he calls "two distant realities." The juxtaposition is made or not made, and that is the long and the short of it. Personally, I absolutely refuse to believe that, in Reverdy's work, images such as

In the brook, there is a song that flows

or:

Day unfolded like a white tablecloth

or:

The world goes back into a sack

reveal the slightest degree of premeditation. In my opinion, it is erroneous to claim that "the mind has grasped the relationship" of two realities in the presence of each other. First of all, it has seized nothing consciously. It is, as it were, from the fortuitous juxtaposi-

tion of the two terms that a particular light has sprung, *the light of the image,* to which we are infinitely sensitive. The value of the image depends upon the beauty of the spark obtained; it is, consequently, a function of the difference of potential between the two conductors. When the difference exists only slightly, as in a comparison, the spark is lacking. Now, it is not within man's power, so far as I can tell, to effect the juxtaposition of two realities so far apart. The principle of the association of ideas, such as we conceive of it, militates against it. Or else we would have to revert to an elliptical art, which Reverdy deplores as much as I. We are therefore obliged to admit that the two terms of the image are not deduced one from the other by the mind for the specific purpose of producing the spark, that they are the simultaneous products of the activity I call surrealist, reason's role being limited to taking note of, and appreciating, the luminous phenomenon.

And just as the length of the spark increases to the extent that it occurs in rarefied gases, the surrealist atmosphere created by automatic writing, which I have wanted to put within the reach of everyone, is especially conducive to the production of the most beautiful images. One can even go so far as to say that in this dizzying race the images appear like the only guideposts of the mind. By slow degrees the mind becomes convinced of the supreme reality of these images. At first limiting itself to submitting to them, it soon realizes that they flatter its reason, and increase its knowledge accordingly. The mind becomes aware of the limitless expanses wherein its desires are made manifest, where the pros and cons are constantly consumed, where its obscurity does not betray it. It goes forward, borne by these images which enrapture it, which scarcely leave it any time to blow upon the fire in its fingers. This is the most beautiful night of all, the *lightning-filled night:* day, compared to it, is night. . . .

The mind which plunges into surrealism relives with glowing excitement the best part of its childhood. For such a mind, it is similar to the certainty with which a person who is drowning reviews once more, in the space of less than a second, all the insurmountable moments of his life. Some may say to me that the parallel is not very encouraging. But I have no intention of encouraging those who

tell me that. From childhood memories, and from a few others, there emanates a sentiment of being unintegrated, and then later of *having gone astray,* which I hold to be the most fertile that exists. It is perhaps childhood that comes closest to one's "real life"; childhood beyond which man has at his disposal, aside from his laissez-passer, only a few complimentary tickets; childhood where everything nevertheless conspires to bring about the effective, risk-free possession of oneself. Thanks to surrealism, it seems that opportunity knocks a second time. It is as though we were still running toward our salvation, or our perdition. In the shadow we again see a precious terror. Thank God, it's still only purgatory. With a shudder, we cross what the occultists call *dangerous territory.* In my wake I raise up monsters that are lying in wait; they are not yet too ill disposed toward me, and I am not lost, since I fear them. Here are "the elephants with the heads of women and the flying lions" which used to make Soupault and me tremble in our boots to meet, here is the "soluble fish" which still frightens me slightly. SOLUBLE FISH, am I not the soluble fish, I was born under the sign of Pisces, and man is soluble in his thought! The flora and fauna of surrealism are inadmissible.

From: André Breton,
Manifesto of Surrealism, *in*
Manifestoes of Surrealism,
*translated by Richard Seaver
and Helen R. Lane, University
of Michigan Press, 1969.*

DALÍ AND PARANOIA-CRITICISM

Dalí even revived the movement's youth by effecting its adoption of his method of analysis known as "paranoia-criticism."

Paranoia, as we know, is delirious interpretation of the world, and of the ego, which is given an exaggerated importance. But what distinguishes this disease from other forms of delirium is a perfect and coherent systematization, the accession of a state of omnipotence which often leads the sufferer, moreover, to megalomania or persecution mania. It naturally assumes a number of forms, coherent from their point of depar-

227

ture, and is accompanied by hallucinations, delirious interpretations of real phenomena. The paranoiac enjoys normal physical health, suffers from no organic disturbance, and yet lives and functions in an alien world. Far from submitting to this world like most "normal" people, he dominates it, molds it according to his desires. Dr. Lacan's thesis, published at this time, greatly interested the surrealists and provided serious confirmation of Dalí's position. . . .

But what would paranoia-*criticism* be? According to Dalí, a spontaneous method of irrational knowledge "based on the critical and systematic objectivation of delirious associations and interpretations.". . .

Where and how is this activity carried out? Everywhere—in the poem, where it is most at its ease, in the painting, which would be merely the "hand-made color photograph of concrete irrationality and of the imaginative world in general," in sculpture, which would be the "hand-made model of concrete irrationality . . . ," etc. It also applies to the cinema, to the history of art, "and even, if necessary, to all kinds of exegesis." Dalí's paranoia-criticism of Millet's *Angelus* and his apologia for Art Nouveau are too well known to need further illustration here.

From: Maurice Nadeau, The History of Surrealism, *translated by Richard Howard, Jonathan Cape, 1968.*

A PARANOIAC-CRITICAL INTERPRETATION OF MILLET'S *ANGELUS*

> As beautiful as the chance encounter, on a dissecting table, of a sewing machine and an umbrella.

It is only too clear that the "illustrative fact" can in no way restrict the flow of my delirious ideas, but on the contrary tends to bring them out. Thus with me it can only be a case of paranoiac illustrations, and I must apologize here for the vulgar pleonasm which that supposes. In fact, as I have often had the pleasure and the patience to repeat to my readers, the paranoiac phenomenon is not only that which combines *par excellence* all the "systematic-associative" factors, but also the one which embodies a more "identical" "psychic-interpretive" illustration. Paranoia is not always confined to being a matter of

"illustration"; it further constitutes the true and unique form of "literal illustration," that is to say "delirious interpretive illustration"—"identity" always appearing *a posteriori* as a factor resulting from "interpretive association."

There is no image which seems to me able to illustrate more "literally," in a more delirious fashion, Lautréamont and the *Chants de Maldoror* in particular, than that which was produced some seventy years ago by that painter of tragic cannibal atavisms, of ancestral and terrifying encounters of sweet, soft, high-quality flesh: I am referring to Jean François Millet, that immeasurably misunderstood painter. It is the thousand-times famous *Angelus* of Millet which in my opinion is equivalent in painting to the well-known and sublime "chance encounter, on a dissecting table, of a sewing machine and an umbrella."

Nothing indeed seems to me able to illustrate this encounter in such an atrocious and hyperevident fashion as the haunting image of the *Angelus*. The *Angelus* is, to my knowledge, the only picture in the world which embodies the immobile presence, the expectant encounter of two beings in a solitary, crepuscular, and mortal setting. The solitary, crepuscular, and mortal setting plays, in the picture, the role of the dissecting table in the poetic text, for not only does life fade away on the horizon but also the fork is plunging into that real and substantial meat which plowed earth has always been for man; it is sinking into it, I say, with that purposeful greed for fertility characteristic of the delectable incisions of the scalpel which, as everyone knows, in dissecting any corpse is under various analytical pretexts merely engaged in a secret search for the synthetic, fertile, and nourishing apple of death; hence that constant dualism which has been felt throughout the ages—food, dining table, plowed earth feeding on the honey-sweet manure of authentic and ammoniac necrophiliac desires—a dualism which leads us finally to consider plowed earth, particularly when aggravated by twilight, as the most lavishly provided of dissecting tables, that which among all others offers us the most genuine and appetizing of corpses, seasoned with that fine and imponderable truffle which is only found in nutritive

dreams constituted by the meat of the tenderized shoulders of Hitlerian and atavistic nurses, and with that exciting, incorruptible salt made from the frenetic, voracious swarming of ants which every authentic, self-respecting "uninterred putrefaction" worthy of its name should consist of. If, as we claim, the "plowed earth" is the most literal and advantageous of all known dissecting tables, the umbrella and the sewing machine would be transposed, in the *Angelus,* into a masculine figure and a feminine figure, and all the uneasiness, all the mystery of the encounter would still come, in my very modest opinion—independently of the unease and the mystery which we now know to be determined by the "place" (plowed earth, dissecting table)—from the authentic peculiarities contained in the two people, in the two objects, from which the whole developmental argument is derived, the whole latent tragedy of the expectant and preliminary encounter. The umbrella—a typically surrealist object with a symbolic function—as a result of its flagrant and well-known phenomenon of erection, would be none other than the masculine figure in the *Angelus* which in the picture, as the reader will do me the favour of remembering, is trying to hide his state of erection—and thereby merely succeeding in drawing attention to it—by the shameful and compromising position of his own hat. Opposite him, the sewing machine, well known as a female symbol, exaggeratedly characterized, goes so far as to invoke the mortal and cannibal virtue of her sewing needle, the activity of which may be identified with that superfine perforation of the praying mantis "emptying" her male, that is to say emptying her umbrella, transforming it into that tormented, flaccid, and depressive victim which every closed umbrella becomes after the magnificence of the amorous, paroxysmal, extended functioning which it recently displayed. It is certain that behind the two tense figures of the *Angelus,* that is to say behind the sewing machine and the umbrella, the gleaners can only continue to gather up indifferently, conventionally, fried eggs (without the frying pan), inkpots, spoons, and all the silverware which the last hours of twilight bestow on this sparkling, exhibitionistic hour, and hardly has a raw cutlet been placed on the head of the male than the outline of a "hungry" Napoleon suddenly forms and stands out in the clouds on the horizon, than we see him impatiently approaching the head of his cavalcade to seek out the cutlet in question, which in reality, in truth, is reserved properly speaking for the needle, finest of the fine, most terrifying of the terrifying, most beautiful of the beautiful, of the spectral, clandestine and vigorously healthy sewing machine.

THE ANGELUS OF MILLET, AS BEAUTIFUL AS THE CHANCE ENCOUNTER, ON A DISSECTING TABLE, OF A SEWING MACHINE AND AN UMBRELLA!
Salvador Dalí

From: Nadeau, Histoire du surréalisme suivi des documents surréalistes, *Editions du Seuil, Paris, 1964*

PURE INTUITION AND REFLECTION IN DALÍ'S WORK

It is precisely to the extent that the artist is able to *reproduce,* to objectivize through painting or any other means the external objects whose painful constraint he experiences, that he largely escapes from these objects and avoids falling into a real psychosis. *Sublimation,* which operates in such cases, seems the simultaneous product, in the case of a trauma, of the need for narcissitic fixation (of a sadistic-anal character) and of the social instincts (the eroticization of fraternal objects) induced to reveal themselves electively at this time.

The great originality of Salvador Dalí is in having shown himself strong enough to participate in this activity both as an actor and as a spectator, to have succeeded in appearing half as judge and half as a party in the action brought by pleasure against reality. It is this which comprises *paranoiac-critical* activity as he has defined it: "spontaneous method of irrational knowledge based on the interpretative-critical association of delirious phenomena." He has succeeded in balancing both within and outside himself the lyrical state founded on pure intuition, which will only accept an ever more intense exploration of sensual pleasure (the concept of the maximum possible eroticization of artistic plea-

sure), and the speculative state founded on reflection which affords satisfactions of a more moderate order, which are nevertheless special and refined enough to embody the principle of pleasure. Naturally, with Dalí, one is dealing with a latent paranoia of the most benign kind, paranoia with isolated stages of delirium (to quote the terminology of Kraepelin), with an unmistakable pattern of development. His first-class intelligence succeeds in linking these stages together after the event, but immediately, gradually rationalizing the distance covered. Visionary experiences, the meaningful falsifications of the memory, the ultrasubjective illicit interpretations which make up the clinical picture of paranoia, provide him with the raw material of his work, he regards them, he offers them as the precious lode to be mined. But they are only the basis for a methodical process of organization and exploitation, which tends to gradually reduce the hostile element in the forms of everyday life and to surmount this hostility *on a universal scale.* Dalí indeed does not lose sight of the fact that the human drama emerges from and is fed especially by the contradiction which exists between natural necessity and logical necessity, two necessities which only succeed in coming together in flashes, revealing in a blinding light which is as quickly extinguished the realm of "objective chance": "Paranoiac-critical activity is a force which organizes and produces objective chance."

The external object, as considered by Dalí from his position of arrestation at the stage of the superego, in which he takes a positive pleasure, is endowed with a symbolic life which surpasses all others and tends to make it the concrete vehicle of humour. This object is in fact divorced from its agreed significance, utilitarian or otherwise, in order to be closely linked to the *ego,* in relation to which it retains a constituent value. "You may be sure that the famous soft watches of Salvador Dalí are nothing more or less than the soft, extravagant, solitary paranoiac-critical Camembert of time and space." In New York, Dalí exhibited a red-painted telephone, the receiver of which was formed by a live lobster (an artistic evocation of the self-mutilatory mechanism of ear-cropping begun by Van Gogh). His attitude in the face of what he calls the "strange bodies" of space is

revealing of his attitude of nondifferentiation of the knowledge of objects and that of beings and is characteristic of the "moral aerodynamism" which has enabled him to realize this rare and spectacular fantasy: "To hire a clean little old woman, in the ultimate state of decrepitude, and exhibit her dressed as a toreador, placing on her head, which has been shaved to receive it, an omelette *fines herbes:* which will tremble as a result of the continuous shaking of the little old woman. One could also put a twenty-franc piece on the omelette."

From: André Breton, Anthologie de l'humour noir, *Jean-Jacques Pauvert Editeur, Paris, 1966*

DALÍ'S ART DISTURBS US

Salvador Dalí's work reflects the artist's total involvement in the Freudian concept of the unconscious as a narrative field. Trivial facts, like daily activities, become important parts of a strange and hallucinatory drama. Oedipus conflicts, childhood obsessions mingle in his hugely varied landscapes of the present to create a disturbing and ambiguous atmosphere. Dalí then intervenes, taking advantage of our timidity, to upset the smooth running of reality as it is generally known. The hidden significance of everyday objects in contrast with their unusual organization disturbs us more perhaps because of our familiarity with these objects than because of their unexpected forms. According to a Freudian principle, it is obvious that reason rationalizes reality for us without any apparent danger. Dalí succeeds in sabotaging the mechanism of this useful and familiar process. To describe his almost incredible landscapes Dalí uses techniques of the twentieth century with a satisfaction at the concentration of intentional neuroses caused thereby. Dalí's hallucinatory realism involves us so much that we are thoroughly disturbed by his art.

From: Luca Venturi, in Dali, *edited by David Larkin, Mondadori, 1975*

Index of
works
illustrated

Self-portrait with Neck of Raphael
1922–23
Oil on canvas
54 × 57 cm (21 × 22½ in)
Private collection, Paris
Page 71

Cadaqués
1922
Oil on canvas
60.5 × 82 cm (24 × 32 in)
Collection Montserrat Dalí,
Barcelona
Pages 72–73

Aunt Ana Sewing in Cadaqués
1916–17
Oil on sackcloth
48 × 62 cm (19 × 24½ in)
Collection Joaquín Vila-Moners,
Figueras
Page 74 (detail)

Self-portrait Splitting into Three
Oil on posterboard
70 × 50 cm (27½ × 19½ in)
Teatro Museo Dalí, Figueras
Page 75

Girls
Circa 1923
Gouache on posterboard
105 × 75 cm (41½ × 29½ in)
Teatro Museo Dalí, Figueras
Page 76

The First Days of Spring
1922–23
India ink and watercolour on paper
21.5 × 15.5 cm (8½ × 6 in)
Collection Ramón Estalella, Madrid
Page 78

Figure of a Woman
Circa 1926
Oil on board (unfinished)
61 × 38 cm (24 × 15 in)
Teatro Museo Dalí, Figueras
Page 79

Purist Still Life
Oil on canvas
100 × 100 cm (39½ × 39½ in)
Teatro Museo Dalí, Figueras
Pages 80–81

"Port d'Alguer"
1925
Oil on canvas
36 × 38 cm (14 × 15 in)
Private collection
Pages 84–85

Woman's Head
1927
Oil on canvas
100 × 100 cm (39½ × 39½ in)
Teatro Museo Dalí, Figueras
Page 88

Girl Seen from Behind
1925
Oil on canvas
108 × 77 cm (42½ × 30½ in)
Museo Español de Arte
Contemporáneo, Madrid
Page 82

Putrefied Birds
Circa 1928
Oil and collage on board
50 × 65 cm (19½ × 25½ in)
Teatro Museo Dalí, Figueras
Page 86

**Girl Seen from Behind Looking Out
of the Window**
1925
Oil on canvas
103 × 74 cm (40½ × 29 in)
Museo Español de Arte
Contemporáneo, Madrid
Page 83

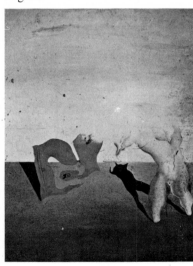

Torso
Circa 1928
Oil on board
76 × 63 cm (30 × 25 in)
Teatro Museo Dalí, Figueras
Page 87

Inaugural Gooseflesh
1928
Oil on canvas
75.5 × 62.5 cm (29½ × 24½ in)
Collection Ramón Pichot, Barcelona
Page 89

Perspective
1936
Oil on canvas
65 × 65.5 cm (25½ × 26 in)
E. Hoffmann Foundation,
Kunstmuseum, Basel
Pages 90–91

Portrait of Gala
1931
Oil on posterboard
14 × 9 cm (5½ × 3½ in)
Collection Albert Field, New York
Page 92

Ghosts of Two Automobiles
Circa 1929
Collage and oil on posterboard
Teatro Museo Dalí, Figueras
Page 93

The Specter of Sex Appeal
1934
Oil on board
17 × 13 cm (6½ × 5 in)
Teatro Museo Dalí, Figueras
Page 94

**Three Young Surrealistic Women
Holding in their Arms the Skins of
an Orchestra**
1936
Oil on canvas
54 × 65 cm (21 × 25½ in)
Salvador Dalí Foundation, Inc.
St. Petersburg, Florida
Pages 96–97

**Soft Construction with Cooked
Beans—Premonition of Civil War**
1936
Oil on canvas
100 × 99 cm (39½ × 39 in)
Collection Louise and Walter
Arensberg, Philadelphia Museum of
Art Pages 93–94

**The Chemist of Figueras Who Is
Looking for Absolutely Nothing**
1936
Oil on wood
30 × 56 cm (12 × 22 in)
Collection Edward F. W. James,
Sussex
Pages 100–01

Geological Justice
1936
Oil on wood
11 × 19 cm (4½ × 7½ in)
Collection Edward F. W. James,
Sussex
Page 102, top

Solar Table
1936
60 × 46 cm (23½ × 18 in)
Edward F. W. James Foundation,
Brighton Art Gallery, Brighton
Page 102, bottom (detail)

Spain
1938
Oil on canvas
92 × 60 cm (36 × 23½ in)
Collection Edward F. W. James,
Sussex
Page 104

Rhinocerontic Gooseflesh
1956
Oil on canvas
93 × 60 cm (36½ × 23½ in)
Collection Bruno Pagliari, Mexico
Page 105

The Infinite Mystery
1938
Oil on cloth
114 × 146 cm (45 × 57½ in)
Private collection, New York
Pages 106–07

Sleep
1937
Oil on canvas
51 × 78 cm (20 × 30½ in)
Collection Edward F. W. James,
Sussex
Page 109 (detail)

Autumn Cannibalism
1936–37
Oil on canvas
80 × 80 cm (31½ × 31½ in)
Collection Edward F. W. James,
Sussex
Page 110 (detail)

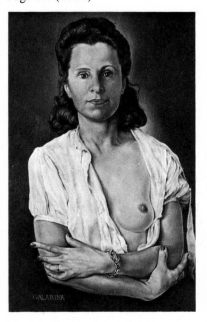

Galarina
1945
Oil on canvas
65 × 50 cm
Teatro Museo Dalí, Figueras
Page 111

Léda Atomica
1949
Oil on canvas
60 × 44 cm (23½ × 17½ in)
Teatro Museo Dalí, Figueras
Pages 112–13

Dalí at the Age of Six When He Thought He Was a Girl, Lifting the Skin of the Water to See a Dog Sleeping in the Shadow of the Sea
1950
Oil on canvas
27 × 34 cm (10½ × 13½ in)
Collection Count François de Vallombreuse, Paris
Pages 114–15

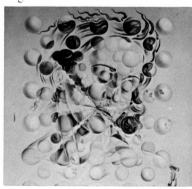

Galatea with Spheres
1952
Oil on canvas
65 × 54 cm (25½ × 21 in)
Private collection, New York
Pages 116–17

The Christ of St. John of the Cross
1951
Oil on canvas
205 × 116 cm (80½ × 45½ in)
Glasgow Art Gallery and Museum
Pages 118–19

The Madonna of Port Lligat
1950
Oil on canvas
366 × 244 cm (144 × 96 in)
Collection Lady J. Dunn, Quebec
Page 120

The Bread Basket
1945
Oil on canvas
37 × 32 cm (14½ × 12½ in)
Teatro Museo Dalí, Figueras
Page 123

Vertigo
1930
Oil on canvas
60 × 50 cm (23½ × 19½ in)
Collection Carlo Ponti, Rome
Page 124 (detail)

The Eye of Time
Jewelled watch
1951–52
The Owen Cheatham Foundation, New York
Page 125, top

Mouth
Brooch of gold, rubies, and pearls
1951–52
The Owen Cheatham Foundation,
New York
Page 125, bottom

Nature Morte Vivante
1956
Oil on cloth
125 × 160 cm (49 × 63 in)
Salvador Dalí Foundation, Inc.
St. Petersburg, Florida
Pages 126–27

**Rhinocerontic Disintegration of
Phidias Ilissos**
1954
Oil on canvas
99 × 129 cm (39 × 51 in)
Private collection, New York
Pages 128–29

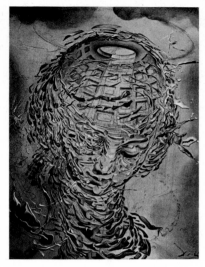

**Exploding Head in the Style of
Raphael**
1951
Oil on canvas
67 × 57 (26 × 22½ in)
Collection Stead H. Stead-Ellis,
Somerset Page 130

The Last Supper
1955
Oil on canvas
167 × 268 cm (65½ × 105½ in)
Collection Chester Dale, National
Gallery of Art, Washington
Pages 132 top (detail at bottom) and
133 (detail)

Gala Looking at Christ Hypercubicus
1954
Oil on canvas
31 × 27 cm (12 × 10½ in)
Teatro Museo Dalí, Figueras
Page 134

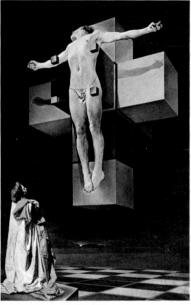

Corpus Hypercubicus
1954
Oil on canvas
194 × 124 cm
Collection Chester Dale,
Metropolitan Museum of Art, New
York
Pages 136–37 and 138 (detail)

Santiago the Great
1957
Oil on canvas
400 × 300 cm (157½ × 118 in)
Collection Lord Beaverbrook,
Fredericton Gallery of Art, Canada
Pages 139 and 140 (detail)

Gala Nude Seen from Behind
1960
Oil on canvas
42 × 32 cm
Teatro Museo Dalí, Figueras
Page 142

Velázquez Painting the Infanta Margarita with the Light and Shadow of His Own Glory
1958
Oil on canvas
153 × 92 cm (60 × 36 in)
Salvador Dalí Foundation, Inc.
St. Petersburg, Florida
Page 143

Stereoscopic Painting
1976
Oil on canvas
Teatro Museo Dalí, Figueras
Pages 144–45

The Discovery of America by Christopher Columbus
1959
Oil on canvas
410 × 310 cm (161½ × 122 in)
Salvador Dalí Foundation, Inc.
St. Petersburg, Florida
Pages 146 and 147, 148–49 and 150–51 (details)

Virgin of Guadalupe
1959
Oil on canvas
130 × 98.5 cm (51 × 38½ in)
Collection Alfonso Fierro, Madrid
Pages 152–53 and 154–55 (detail)

Battle of Tetuán
1962
Oil on canvas
308 × 406 cm (121 × 160 in)
Collection David Nahonad, Milan
Pages 156 and 157, 158–59, 160–61 (details)

Salvador Dalí in the Act of Painting Gala in the Apotheosis of the Dollar, in Which Can Also Be Seen, on the Left, Marcel Duchamp Disguised as Louis XIV, Behind a Curtain in the Style of Vermeer Which Is None Other Than the Invisible but Monumental Face of the Hermes of Praxiteles
1965
Oil on canvas
400 × 498 cm (157½ × 196 in)
Private collection, New York
Pages 163 and 164 (detail)

The Christ of El Vallés
1962
Oil on canvas
92 × 75 cm (36 × 29½ in)
Collection Dr. Giuseppe Albaretto,
Turin Page 165

Portrait of My Dead Brother
1963
Oil on canvas
175 × 175 cm (69 × 69 in)
Private collection, New York
Pages 166–67

**Gala Contemplating Dalí in a State of
Levitation Above His "Pop, Op, Yes,
Yes, Pompier" Work of Art in Which
We Can See the Two Anxious
Characters from Millet's *Angelus* in
an Atavistic State of Hibernation in
Front of a Sky Which Can Suddenly
Transform Itself into a Gigantic
Maltese Cross, in the Very Center of
Perpignan Station, on Which the
Whole Universe Is Converging**
1965
Oil on canvas
295 × 406 cm (116 × 160 in)
Private collection, New York
Pages 168–69

Pen and Ink Drawing
1970
Teatro Museo Dalí, Figueras
Page 170

Hallucinogenic Toreador
1969–70
Oil on canvas
400 × 300 cm (157½ × 118 in)
Salvador Dalí Foundation, Inc.
St. Petersburg, Florida
Page 171

Tuna Fishing
1966–67
Oil on canvas
304 × 404 cm (119½ × 159 in)
Paul Ricard Foundation, Paris
Pages 173 and 174, 175 (details)

Portrait of Gala
1969
Pen and ink drawing
Teatro Museo Dalí, Figueras
Page 177

Ruggero Liberating Angelica
1974
Oil on canvas
Teatro Museo Dalí, Figueras
Page 178, left

Anchorite
1974
Oil on canvas
Teatro Museo Dalí, Figueras
Pages 178–79

Explosion of Faith in a Cathedral
1974
Oil on canvas
Teatro Museo Dalí, Figueras
Pages 180 and 182 (detail)

Transformation
1974
Oil on canvas
Teatro Museo Dalí, Figueras
Page 185

Figure Seen from Behind
1974
Gouache
Teatro Museo Dalí, Figueras
Page 179, right

Angels Watching the Ordination of a Saint
1974
Pen and ink drawing
Teatro Museo Dalí, Figueras
Page 183

Putrefied Bird
Circa 1928
Oil on board
37.5 × 57 cm (15 × 22½ in)
Teatro Museo Dalí, Figueras
Pages 186–87

Naked Torso
Circa 1928
Oil on board
79.5 × 38.5 cm (31 × 15 in)
Teatro Museo Dalí, Figueras
Page 187, left